Alan Dunn

creative
cakes

NEW
HOLLAND

Dedication
Thank you to Sathyavathi Narayanswamy, Christiane Duclos, Vivien and Yongtae Lee, Tombi Peck, Alice Christie, Andrew Lockey, Stacey and Graeme Veitch, Jay Aston, Cheryl Baker and Mike Nolan, Allen and Avril Dunn, Susan and Mark Laird, Margaret Carter, Norma Laver and Jenny Walker, Beverley Dutton, John Quai Hoi, Simona Hill and Sue Atkinson.

First published in 2012 by New Holland Publishers (UK) Ltd
London • Cape Town • Sydney • Auckland
www.newhollandpublishers.com

Garfield House	Wembley Square	Unit 1, 66 Gibbes Street	218 Lake Road
86–88 Edgware Road	Solan Street, Gardens	Chatswood	Northcote
London W2 2EA, UK	Cape Town 8000	New South Wales 2067	Auckland
	South Africa	Australia	New Zealand

10 9 8 7 6 5 4 3 2 1

ISBN 978 1 78009 044 3

Publisher: Fiona Schultz
Publishing Director: Lliane Clarke
Senior Editor: Simona Hill
Photographer: Sue Atkinson
Designer: Kimberley Pearce
Production Director: Olga Dementiev

Printed and bound
Toppan Leefung Printing Ltd (China)

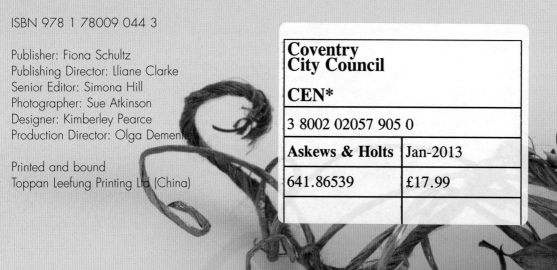

Contents

Introduction

I have been cake decorating and sugarcrafting since I was 14 years old. My grandfather had been a baker by trade – working in a bakery part time from the age of seven, and full time at the age of 12, and eventually owning his own business. Although he had retired from the trade by the time I had taken an interest, the seeds had been planted. I had grown up in an environment where his simply iced cakes, together with my mother's weekend baking, were part of everyday life. Like my grandfather I trained as a baker and confectioner, studying for the City & Guilds 120 and 121 qualifications when I left school at 16. It was during this period that I joined The British Sugrcraft Guild following the advice of my first tutor Margaret Morland (now Carter). The Guild had been set up in 1981 by a group of enthusiastic cake decorators. Tombi Peck, one of the founder members, brought together a group of like-minded people with the aim of sharing knowledge and spreading the word about this creative craft.

It was through my early college classes and attendance at monthly guild meetings that I soon realised that cake decorating could be a much more creative process than the cake designs I remembered from my childhood. Better still, it could be an art form. I would later become one of Tombi's students. At that early stage in my learning I never considered that one day I would teach alongside Tombi.

Although I have always been interested in all areas of cake decorating it is the art of sugar flowers that has fuelled my passion for the craft. Flowers can be very time consuming to make, and not always cost effective for those wanting a quick cake design, though I'm not sure that a quick cake design exists.

When I was asked to write this book, it was intended that several of the cake designs would be simpler than those featured in my previous titles, as well as including several cakes without my usual signature flowers. With this in mind I have created cakes that will take a day or even half a day to make - though each maintains that creative attention to detail for which I always strive. Of course, there are many designs that will take much longer – those designs that include my signature sugar flowers are more time consuming to create.

Materials

The materials listed here are essential for making and decorating sugar flowers. Begin with a few well-chosen colours and build up a collection as time and budget permits.

CONFECTIONER'S VARNISH

This product can be used neat to create a high glaze on berries and foliage. I mostly dilute the glaze with isopropyl alcohol (often sold as dipping solution or glaze cleaner in cake decorating shops). This lessens the shine, giving a more natural effect. I mix the two liquids together in a clean glass with a lid. Do not shake it as this produces air bubbles. Leaves can be dipped straight into the glaze, shaking off the excess before hanging to dry or placing onto kitchen paper to blot off any excess. The glaze can also be painted onto the leaf but I find the bristles pull off some of the dust colour, giving a streaky effect. A build-up of glaze can give a streaky shiny finish which is undesirable. I use various strengths of glaze:

- ¾-glaze (1 part isopropyl alcohol to 3 parts confectioner's varnish) gives a high glaze but without a 'plastic' finish left by undiluted confectioner's varnish.
- ½-glaze (equal proportions of the two). This is used to give a natural shine for many types of foliage, including ivy and rose leaves.
- ¼-glaze (3 parts isopropyl alcohol to 1 part confectioner's varnish). This is used for leaves and sometimes petals that don't require a shine but just need something stronger than steaming to set the colour and remove the dusty finish.

When the varnish has dried, you might like to use a craft knife to scratch or etch through the glaze into the surface of the flowerpaste to create fine white veins on some leaves.

CORNFLOUR BAG

An essential if you have hot hands! Cornflour is a lifesaver when the flowerpaste is sticky. Make a cornflour bag using disposable nappy liners; these can be bought from most large chemists. Fold a couple of layers of nappy liners together and put a generous tablespoon of cornflour on top. Tie the nappy liner into a bag using ribbon or an elastic band. Use the bag to lightly dust the paste prior to rolling it out and to dust petals or leaves before putting them into a veiner.

CRAFT DUSTS

These are inedible and only intended for items that are not going to be eaten. Craft dusts are much stronger and more light-fast than food colour dusts. Care must be taken as they tend to migrate the moment the lid is taken off the pot. Dust in an enclosed space as once these colours get into the air they have a habit of landing where you don't want them. To prevent spotty cakes, it is best to keep them in boxes while you are dusting the flowers.

EDIBLE GLAZE SPRAY

There are several ways to glaze leaves. I use an edible spray varnish made by Fabilo. This glaze can be used lightly for most leaves or sprayed in layers for shiny leaves and berries. Spray in a well-ventilated area, perhaps wearing a filter mask. Spraying leaves is much quicker than the method below which I also use from time to time.

EGG WHITE

You will need fresh egg white to stick petals together and to alter the consistency of paste if it is too dry. Many cake decorators avoid fresh egg white because of salmonella fears. Edible glues can be used instead, if you prefer, but I find that these dissolve the sugar slightly before allowing it to dry, resulting in weak flower petals.

LIQUID COLOURS

These are generally used to colour royal icing as they alter the consistency of flowerpaste, sugarpaste and almond paste but they can also be great to paint with. I use a small selection of liquid colours to paint fine spots and fine lines on to petals. I mostly use cyclamen and poinsettia red liquid colours for flower-making.

PASTE FOOD COLOURS

I use only a small selection of paste food colours and prefer to work with white or a very pale base colour and then create stronger finished colours using powder food colours. I add paste colours to sugarpaste to cover the cakes but am not a huge fan. It is best to mix up a small ball of sugarpaste with some paste food colour and then add this ball to the larger amount of paste – this will help avoid adding too much colour to the entire amount of sugarpaste.

PETAL DUSTS

These food colour dusts contain gum that helps them adhere to the petal or leaf. They are wonderful for creating very soft and intense colouring on finished flowers. Dusts can be mixed together to form new colours or brushed on in layers, which creates interest and depth to the finished flower or leaf. White petal dust can be added to soften the colours; some cake decorators add cornflour but I find this weakens the gum content of the dust, often causing a streaky effect on the petal. If you want to create bold, strong colours dust the surface of the flowerpaste while it is still fairly pliable or at the leather-hard stage. A paint can also be made by adding clear alcohol (isopropyl) to the dust. This is good for adding spots and finer details. You can also add this dust to melted cocoa butter to make a 'paint' that can be used to create designs on the surface of a cake. Petal dusts can be used in small amounts to colour flowerpaste to create interesting and subtle base colours.

WHITE VEGETABLE FAT

I use this to grease non-stick boards and then wipe it off with dry kitchen paper. This does two things: it conditions the board, helping prevent the flowerpaste from sticking to it, and also removes excess food colour that might have been left on the board. Add a tiny amount of white fat to flowerpaste if it is very sticky. However, if you add too much it will make the paste short and slow down the drying process. Take care not to leave too much fat on the board as greasy patches will show on the petals when you apply the dry dust colours.

Equipment

There is a huge array of sugarcraft equipment for sale. The following are a variety of items that I consider to be the most useful.

BRUSHES

Good-quality synthetic brushes or synthetic-blend brushes from the art shop are best for flower-colouring. I use mainly short, flat, not too soft bristle brushes for applying layers of food colour dusts to flowers and leaves. I keep brushes for certain colours so that I don't need to wash them quite so regularly. I use finer sable or synthetic-blend brushes for painting fine lines or detail spots onto petals.

CELSTICKS (CC/CELCAKES)

Celsticks come in four sizes and are ideal for rolling out small petals and leaves and for creating thick ridges.

The pointed end of the tool is great for opening up the centre of 'hat'-type flowers. The rounded end can be used in the same way as a ball tool, to soften edges and hollow out petals.

CERAMIC TOOLS (HP/HOLLY PRODUCTS)

A smooth ceramic tool is used for curling the edges of petals and hollowing out throats of small flowers, as well as serving the purpose of a mini rolling pin. Another of the ceramic tools, known as the silk-veining tool, is wonderful for creating delicate veins and frills to petal edges.

DRESDEN/VEINING TOOL (J OR PME)

The fine end of this tool is great for adding central veins to petals or leaves, and the broader end can be used for working the edges of a leaf to give a serrated effect or a 'double-frilled' effect on the edges of petals. Simply press the tool against the paste repeatedly to create a tight frilled effect or pull the tool against the paste on a non-stick board to create serrations. The fine end of the tool can also be used to cut into the edge of the paste to cut and flick finer serrated-edged leaves. I use a black tool by Jem for finer, smaller leaves and flowers, and the larger yellow PME tool for larger flowers.

FOAM PADS

Place petals and leaves on foam pads while you soften the edges – especially if you have hot hands that tend to dissolve the petals as you are working them. Prior to buying this product, check that it has a good surface as some have a rough-texture that will tear the edges of petals or leave marks on them. I like the large blue pad, Billy's block, or the yellow celpad.

GLUE

Non-toxic glue sticks can be bought from stationery or art shops and are great for fixing ribbon to the cake drum's edge. Always make sure that the glue does not come into direct contact with the cake. I use a hi-tack non-toxic craft glue to attach stamens to the end of wires. No harm is done when

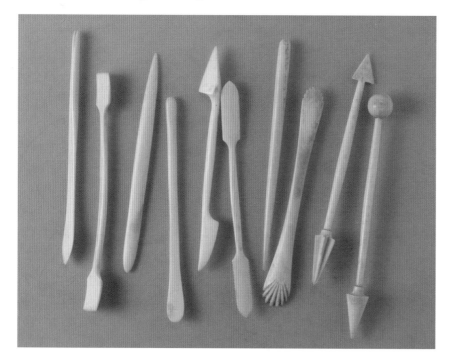

sticking inedible items together with other inedible items. However, the glue should not come into direct contact with the sugar petals as it will dissolve them.

KITCHEN PAPER RING FORMERS
These are great for holding and supporting petals to create a cupped shape as they dry allowing the paste/petal to breathe, which speeds up the drying process (plastic formers tend to slow down the drying process). To make, cut a strip of kitchen paper, twist it, then tie it in a loop, or for larger petals, cut a sheet of kitchen paper diagonally across, twist and tie.

METAL BALL TOOLS (CC/CELCAKES)
I use mostly metal ball tools to work the edges of petals and leaves. These are heavier than plastic ball tools, which means that less effort is needed to soften the paste. I mostly work the tool using a rubbing or rolling action against the paste, positioning it half on the petal/leaf edge and half on my hand or foam pad that the petal is resting

against. It can also be used to 'cup' or hollow out petals to form interesting shapes.

NON-STICK BOARD

This is an essential addition to the flower-maker's workbox. Avoid white boards as they make the eyes strain too much. Some boards can be very shiny, making it difficult to frill the petals against them. If this is the case, simply roughen up the surface using some fine glass paper prior to use or turn over the board and use the back, which is often less shiny. I always apply a thin layer of white vegetable fat rubbed into the surface of the board, then remove most of the excess with dry kitchen paper – this stops the paste sticking to the board and also makes you check each time to see if it is clean from food colour.

PETAL, FLOWER AND LEAF CUTTERS AND VEINERS

There is a huge selection of metal and plastic petal, flower and leaf cutters available from cake decorating shops. Petal and leaf moulds/veiners are made from food-grade silicone rubber. They are very useful for creating natural petal and leaf textures on sugar work. The moulds have been made using mostly real plant material, giving the finished sugar flower a realistic finish. There is an impressive selection of commercial veiners to choose from.

PLAIN-EDGED CUTTING WHEEL (PME) AND CRAFT KNIFE

This is rather like a small double-sided pizza wheel. It is great for cutting out petals and leaves quickly, and also for adding division lines to buds. A craft knife is essential for marking veins, adding texture and cutting petal shapes.

POSY PICKS

These are made from food-grade plastic and come in various sizes. They are used to hold the handle of a spray or bouquet of flowers in the cake. The food-grade plastic protects the cake from contamination by the wires and floristry tape used in the construction of floral sprays. Never push wires directly into a cake.

ROLLING PINS

It's good to have a selection of non-stick rolling pins in various sizes. They are essential for rolling out flowerpaste, sugarpaste and almond paste.

SCISSORS, PLIERS AND WIRE CUTTERS

Fine embroidery and curved scissors are very useful for cutting fine petals, thread and ribbons. Larger florist's scissors are useful for cutting wires and ribbon. Small, fine-nosed pliers are another essential. Good-quality pliers from electrical supply shops are best – they are expensive but worth the investment. Electrical wire cutters are useful for cutting heavier wires.

STAMENS AND THREAD

There is a huge selection of commercial stamens available from cake decorating shops. I use mainly fine white and seed-head stamens, which I can then colour using powder colours. Fine cotton thread is best for stamens. I use lace-making Brock 120 white thread, although some thicker threads may also be useful for larger flowers. An emery board is great for fluffing up the tips of the thread to forms anthers.

TWEEZERS

It is important to use fine, angled tweezers without ridges (or teeth).

They are useful for pinching ridges on petals and holding very fine petals and stamens. They are also very handy when arranging flowers to push smaller items into difficult, tight areas of an arrangement or spray.

WIRES AND FLORISTRY TAPE

I buy mostly white paper-covered wires, preferring to colour or tape over as I work. The quality varies between brands. The most consistent quality are Japanese Sunrise wires. These are available from 35-gauge (very fine but rare) to 18-gauge (thicker). Floristry tape is used in the construction of stems and bouquets. They contain a glue that is released when the tape is stretched. I use mainly nile green, brown and white from the Lion Brand tape company.

TAPE SHREDDER

This tool contains three razor blades to cut floristry tape into quarter-widths. I have a couple of tape shredders and have removed two blades from one of them so that it cuts the tape into half-widths. I rub a tiny amount of cold cream onto the blades with a cotton bud and also a little onto the lid that presses against the blades – this helps the tape run smoothly against the blades as it can often stick to an excess of glue left behind from the tape. Remove any build-up of glue from the blades using fine-nosed pliers. Replace the blades regularly. Handle with care at all times.

Recipes

The following recipes are all used to make the cakes featured in this book. A rich fruit cake that is traditionally made for celebration cakes.

Sunshine Fruit Cake

This is a fabulous and flavourful option for those who prefer a lighter cake. The white chocolate gives a very pleasant aftertaste.

INGREDIENTS

150 g (5½ oz/1¼ cups) glacé cherries (multi-coloured ones look great), halved, washed and allowed to dry
100 g (3½ oz/1 cup) ground almonds
100 g (3½ oz/1 cup) each of dried ready-to-eat pineapple, mango, peach, apricot and pear
1 medium Bramley apple, grated
50 g (2 oz/2 squares) grated white chocolate
75 g (2½ oz/¾ cup) dried cranberries
45 ml (3 tbsp) brandy (optional)
225 g (8 oz/1 cup) unsalted butter, at room temperature
225 g (8 oz/1 cup) caster sugar
1 tsp salt
4 large eggs
250 g (9 oz/2 cups) plain flour mixed with ¼ level tsp baking powder
5 ml (1 tsp) vanilla extract

1. Preheat the oven to 180°C/350°F/Gas mark 4. Line a 20 cm (8 in) round cake tin with greaseproof paper.

2. Toss the glacé cherries in the ground almonds and set aside. Chop the remaining exotic fruits and then toss them with the grated apple, white chocolate, dried cranberries and brandy. Leave for an hour or so.

3. In a separate bowl, beat the butter, sugar and salt together until pale and fluffy. Beat in the eggs, one at a time, alternating with a tablespoon of flour and beating well between each addition. Stir in the remaining flour and vanilla extract. Then add the exotic fruit mixture and the cherries with the ground almonds and stir well to incorporate the fruit.

4. Spoon the mixture into the prepared cake tin. Level the top and bake for 30 minutes, then turn the oven temperature down to 150°C/300°F/ Gas mark 3 and continue to bake for 1½–2 hours. Cover the cake with foil if you think the cake is catching or turn the oven temperature down a little. Leave the cake to cool in the tin before turning out. The cake is ready when a skewer inserted into the centre comes out clean.

Fruit Cake

Double the quantities for a three-tier wedding cake and line another small tin just in case there is some cake mixture left over. This recipe will fill a 30 cm (12 in) round cake tin, plus a little extra for a smaller cake. If I only need a 20 cm (8 in) oval cake I still make up this full quantity and bake extra cakes with the remaining mixture – it's hardly worth turning the oven on just for one small cake. The variety and amount of each dried fruit can be changed to suit your personal preference.

INGREDIENTS

1 kg (2 lb 3 oz/8 cups) raisins
1 kg (2 lb 3 oz/8 cups) sultanas
500 g (1 lb 2 oz/4 cups) dried figs, chopped
500 g (1 lb 2 oz/4 cups) prunes, chopped
250 g (9 oz/2 cups) natural colour glacé cherries, halved
125 g (4½ oz/1 cup) dried apricots, chopped
125 g (4½ oz/1 cup) dried or glacé pineapple, chopped
Grated zest and juice of 1 orange
200 ml (7 fl oz/1½ cup) brandy
500 g (1 lb 2 oz/2 cups) unsalted butter, at room temperature
250 g (9 oz/2 cups) light muscovado sugar
250 g (9 oz/2 cups) dark muscovado sugar
4 tsp apricot jam
8 tsp golden syrup
1 tsp each of ground ginger, allspice, nutmeg, cloves and cinnamon
½ tsp mace
500 g (1 lb 2 oz/4 cups) plain flour
250 g (9 oz/2 cups) ground almonds
10 large eggs, at room temperature

1. Mix the dried fruit, orange zest and juice, and alcohol together in a plastic container with a lid. Seal the container and leave to soak overnight.

2. Preheat the oven to 140°C/275°F/Gas mark 1. Cream the butter in a large bowl until soft. Gradually add the two types of sugar and beat together.

3. Stir in the apricot jam, golden syrup, spices and mace.

4. Sieve the flour into a separate bowl and stir in the almonds.

5. In another bowl, beat the eggs then add slowly to the butter/sugar mixture, alternating it with the flour/almond mix. Do not add the eggs too quickly as the mixture may curdle.

6. Set aside a small amount of batter – this will be used on top of the fruited batter to stop the fruit catching on the top in the oven. Mix the soaked fruit into the remaining batter. Grease and line the tin(s) with baking parchment. Fill the tin to the required depth – I usually aim for about two-thirds the depth of the tin. Apply a thin layer of the un-fruited batter on top and smooth over. Bake for 4–6 hours, depending on the size of the cake. When ready the cake should shrink slightly from the sides of the tin, be firm to the touch and smell wonderful. If in doubt test with a skewer – if it comes out clean the cake is ready.

7. Allow the cake to cool slightly in the tin, add a couple of extra dashes of alcohol, and leave to go cold before removing from the tin. Store wrapped in non-stick parchment paper and plastic wrap. Allow to mature for as long as you have – a few days to a few months works well.

Bucks Fizz Cupcakes

Named after the Eurovision winning band and the cocktail, these decadent cupcakes are flavoured with champagne and orange juice, making them a truly special addition to a celebration. Make one large cake if you like.

INGREDIENTS
200 g (7 oz/1¾ cups) plain flour
3 eggs, separated
200 g (7 oz/scant 1 cup) caster sugar
2 orange zests
1 tsp baking powder
20 ml (4 tbsp) orange juice
20 ml (4 tbsp) champagne

BUTTERCREAM
250 g (9 oz/1¼ cups) unsalted butter
300 g (11 oz/3 cups) icing sugar
Juice of 1 orange
Champagne, to taste

1. Preheat the oven to 160°C /320°F/Gas mark 3. Grease and lightly flour a 23cm (9 in) cake tin, or line a muffin mould with paper liners.

2. In a mixing bowl, beat the egg yolks with the sugar and orange zest until light and fluffy. Sift over flour and baking powder and beat well to combine.

3. In a large clean, non-metallic bowl, beat the egg whites to stiff peaks with a clean wire whisk or electric beater. Fold the egg whites into the batter.

4. Pour the batter into the prepared cake tin and bake for 50 minutes to 1 hour. Bake little cupcakes for 10–12 minutes, or 15 minutes for the muffins.

5. Remove from the oven and leave to cool on a wire rack. Spoon over a little of the orange juice and champagne onto each cake.

BUCKS FIZZ BUTTERCREAM:
6. Cream the butter with the icing sugar until light and fluffy. Beat in the orange juice and add the champagne slowly, to taste. Swirl generously on the top of each cake.

Royal Icing

This recipe is ideal for small amounts of royal icing required to create brush embroidery, lace, embroidery and other piped techniques.

INGREDIENTS
1 medium egg white, at room temperature
225 g (8 oz/1¾ cups) icing sugar, sifted

1. Place the egg white into a clean grease-free bowl of an electric mixer with the majority of the icing sugar and mix the two together with a metal spoon.

2. Fix the bowl and beater to the machine and beat on the lowest speed until the icing has reached full peak – this takes about 8 minutes. You may need to add a little extra sugar if the mixture is too soft.

Flowerpaste

I always buy ready-made commercial flowerpaste (APOC) as it tends to be more consistent than homemade pastes. The following recipe is the one I used prior to discovering commercial flowerpaste! Gum tragacanth gives the paste stretch and strength.

INGREDIENTS
5 tsp cold water
2 tsp powdered gelatine
500 g (1 lb 2 oz/3 cups) icing sugar, sifted
3 tsp gum tragacanth
2 tsp liquid glucose
4 tsp white vegetable fat
1 large fresh egg white

1. Mix the cold water and gelatine together in a small bowl and leave to stand for 30 minutes. Sift the icing sugar and gum tragacanth together into the bowl of a heavy-duty mixer and fit to the machine.

2. Place the bowl with the gelatine mixture over a pan of hot water and stir until the gelatine dissolves. Warm a teaspoon in hot water and then add the liquid glucose together with 1 tablespoon of white fat to the gelatine mixture, and continue to heat until dissolved and thoroughly mixed together.

3. Add the dissolved gelatine mixture to the icing sugar/gum tragacanth with the egg white. Beat at the mixer's lowest speed, then gradually increase the speed to maximum until the paste is white and stringy.

4. Remove the paste from the bowl, knead into a smooth ball and cover with the remaining teaspoon of white fat – this helps to prevent the paste forming a dry crust that can leave hard bits in the paste at the rolling out stage. Place in a plastic food bag and store in an airtight container. Allow the paste to rest and mature for 12 hours before use.

5. Knead the paste well before using it, otherwise it may dry out and crack at the edges. This is an air-drying paste so when you're not using it make sure it is well wrapped in plastic. If you cut out lots of petals, cover them with plastic.

Cold Porcelain

This is an inedible air-drying craft paste. Flowers made from it are much stronger and less prone to break than those made with flowerpaste. However, because it is inedible, anything made from this paste cannot come into direct contact with a cake's surface, so flowers made from cold porcelain need to be placed in a container. There are several commercial cold porcelain pastes available but you can make your own. Use measuring spoons and cups for accurate results and keep all equipment specially for the purpose.

INGREDIENTS
37.5 ml (2½ tbsp) baby oil
115 ml (4 fl oz/½ cup) non-toxic
hi-tack craft glue (Impex)
115 ml (4 fl oz/½ cup) white PVA
wood glue (Liberon Super Wood
Glue or Elmers Glue)
125 g (4½ oz/1 cup) cornflour
Permanent white artist's gouache paint

1. Work in a well-ventilated area when making this paste. Wear a filter mask if you suffer from asthma. Put the baby oil and the two glues in a non-stick pan and mix to form an emulsion. Stir in the cornflour. It will go lumpy.

2. Place the pan over a medium heat and stir the paste with a heavy-duty plastic or wooden spoon. The paste will gradually come away from the base and sides of the pan to form a ball around the spoon. Scrape any uncooked paste from the spoon and add it to the mix. The cooking time will vary – usually around 10 minutes – but the general rule is the lower the heat and the slower you mix the paste, then the smoother the resulting paste will be. Keep stirring the paste to cook it evenly, ensuring the inner parts of the ball cook too – be careful not to overcook the mixture.

3. Turn the paste onto a non-stick board and knead until smooth. It is quite hot at this stage. The kneading helps distribute heat through the paste to cook any undercooked areas. If the paste is very sticky put it back in the pan to cook for longer. It is better if it is slightly undercooked as you can always add heat later – if the paste is overcooked then it is almost impossible to work with.

4. Wrap in cling film and leave to cool – moisture will build up on the surface of the paste which, if left, will encourage mould growth, so it is important to knead the paste when cool and then re-wrap it. Place in a plastic food bag and then in an airtight container, and store at room temperature. This paste has been known to work well two years after it was made if correctly stored.

5. Prior to making flowers you will need to add a smidge of permanent white gouache paint to the paste, which makes the finished flowers more opaque. Although the paste looks white it dries clear, giving a translucence to the finished flower. The paste is similar to sugar to work with except I use cold cream cleanser instead of white vegetable fat, and glue or anti-bacterial wipes/water to moisten the petals to stick them. Cornflour is used as for handling flowerpaste. The paste shrinks a little as it dries – this is because of the glue. This can be disconcerting to begin with but you'll gradually get used to it and it can be an advantage when making miniature flowers.

Techniques

The following techniques are all essential to making and decorating cakes with sprays of flowers. Master these preparation skills and the rest will follow.

Coating a Cake with Almond Paste

Almond paste is applied in one even layer to a cake. It is an important stage because it affects the layers of sugarpaste and decoration that follow.

1. Before applying any form of coating to a cake, it must be level. If a dome has formed during baking then carefully cut it off the top of the cake. Turn the cake upside down so that the flat bottom becomes the cake top. Fill any large indentations with almond paste.

2. Place the cake onto a thin cake board the same size as the cake so that it is easier to move. You might also prefer to add a strip of almond paste around the base of the cake to seal it and the cake board tightly together.

3. Warm some apricot jam with a dash of water, brandy or Cointreau, and then sieve it into a bowl to make an apricot glaze that can be painted onto the surface of the cake. This will help to stick the almond paste to the cake and seal the cake to keep it fresh. Apricot glaze is not too dark and the flavour doesn't fight with the taste of the cake or almond paste. Ready-sieved apricot glaze can be bought.

4. Store the almond paste in a warm place prior to using to help soften it slightly. Knead the paste on a clean, dry surface to make it pliable.

5. Rolling out almond paste to an even thickness can be tricky, and a novice might find a pair of marzipan spacers useful to roll against. Lightly dust the work surface with icing sugar. Place the almond paste on top and position the spacers on each side of the paste. Using a non-stick rolling pin long enough to roll out the almond paste to cover at least a 30 cm (12 in) cake, roll the paste out lengthways. Turn it 90 degrees and reposition the spacers on each side. Continue to roll and turn the paste until it is large enough to cover the cake. Use a measuring tape or string to gauge the exact size of the cake top and its sides. Roll the marzipan slightly larger than the size you think you need, especially for awkward-shaped cakes or anything with corners.

6. Plastic smoothers are also essential to create a professional finish: a curved smoother for the top of the cake and a square-edged one for the sides. Using a round-edged plastic smoother, polish and smooth out the surface of the almond

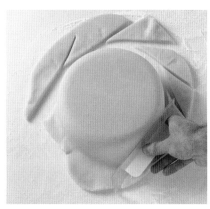
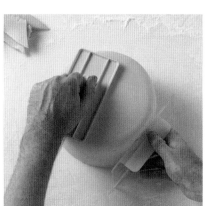

paste. Start gently, gradually increasing the pressure to even out any slightly uneven areas of the paste.

7. Put the rolling pin on top of the almond paste close to one end. Roll the marzipan on to the rolling pin and use the rolling pin to help lift the paste over the cake. Remove the rolling pin and ease the almond paste into place.

8. Smooth the surface of the cake with a smoother to exclude any air bubbles. Tuck the paste down the side of the cake to neatly fit the sides. If you are working on a cake with corners, then concentrate on these first of all.

9. Use the curved-edge smoother to polish the top of the cake. Use strong, firm hand movements to 'iron out' any imperfections.

10. Use the edge of the straight-edged smoother to cut and flick away the excess paste from the base of the cake. Finally, use the same smoother to iron out the sides of the cake using a fair amount of pressure.

11. Place the cake onto a sheet of greaseproof paper and, if time allows, leave to firm up overnight or for a few days prior to coating with sugarpaste.

Coating a Cake and Drum with Sugarpaste

Covering a cake with sugarpaste is a fairly straightforward process – however, practice is needed to achieve very neat results. You will need straight-edge and curved-edge smoothers and a long rolling pin.

1. If you want coloured sugarpaste use paste food colour or thicken liquid colours with icing sugar. It is safer to colour a small amount of sugarpaste and then knead this into the larger amount of paste to control the depth of colour rather than create a paste that is too brightly coloured.

2. Knead the sugarpaste on a clean, dry surface until smooth and pliable. Take care not to knead in too many air bubbles. Lightly dust the work surface with sieved icing sugar and place the sugarpaste on top, with any cracks against the work surface. Roll out, smooth and polish the paste as for almond paste.

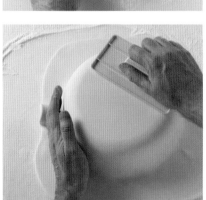

3. Moisten the surface of the almond paste with clear alcohol (Cointreau, kirsch or white rum). Using a sponge apply the alcohol in an even covering. If you leave dry areas it will encourage air bubbles to be trapped between the almond paste and the sugarpaste. The alcohol helps to adhere the sugarpaste to the almond paste and also acts as an antibacterial agent.

4. Pick up the sugarpaste onto the rolling pin and lower it over the cake, taking care to position the paste so that it will cover the sides evenly. Use your hands and then the round-edged smoother to create a smooth finish and eliminate air bubbles.

5. Lift and ease the paste against the sides of the cake. If the cake has corners or points, deal with these first as they often crack or tear. Be careful not to stretch the sugarpaste too much as you work. Trim the excess paste from the base of the cake using a flat knife or the edge of a straight-edged smoother. Use the same smoother to iron out the sides of the cake. Use a pin to prick any air bubbles/pockets that might appear and then smooth over with the sugarpaste smoothers. Use the curved-edge smoother on the top of the cake and the straight-edged smoother on the sides to create a good, even finish.

6. To coat a cake drum, roll out the sugarpaste and carefully place it over a drum moistened with clear alcohol. Smooth over with the round-edged smoother and then trim off the excess with a flat knife. Smooth the cut edge with a smoother to neaten it. Next, polish with a pad of sugarpaste pressed into your palm.

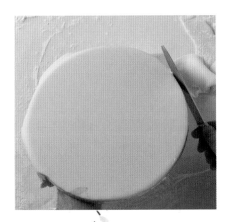

Making a Leaf or Petal Veiner Mould

There are many leaf and petal veiners available to purchase - however, you may wish to make your own, for example, if you are making an unusual flower or leaf. Use mould-making mediums that are non toxic and suitable for food items. The product used here can be purchased from most good art and craft shops. It dries fairly fast and produces consistent results - however, it is an expensive product. Choose leaves and petals that have strong veins – many petals and leaves develop stronger veining as they age.

MATERIALS
Silicone putty (Siligum) kit
Fresh leaf or petal
Facial cold-cream cleanser

EQUIPMENT
Non-stick board
Plastic bags
Measuring spoons
Sharp scissors
Craft knife or scriber

1. There are two compounds in the kit to make silicone putty. The white material is the base and the blue is the catalyst. Once you mix the two together you have to work quickly because it starts to set within 10–20 minutes, depending upon the temperature of the room. This product has a tendency to stick to surfaces so work on a thick plastic board or a food grade plastic bag.

2. Use a measuring spoon to scoop equal amounts of the blue and white compounds onto the work surface. Mix only enough to make the number of veiners you require as, once mixed, the reaction cannot be reversed. Clean the spoon after taking a scoop to avoid contaminating and 'setting' areas of the remaining compounds.

3. Mix the two compounds together thoroughly trying not to knead in too many air bubbles. Press the silicone onto a plastic bag or sheet of plastic and then press the back of the petal or leaf into it, taking care to press the surface evenly in order to avoid air bubbles, which will create a fault in the finished veiner. Leave to set firmly.

4. When the compound has set, simply peel off the leaf or petal. Use sharp scissors to trim away any excess silicone from around the edge of the mould and to tidy the edge. Often the veining on the top half of a leaf or petal is slightly different from the back, so you may decide to leave the leaf or petal in the first half of the veiner and then take a cast of the upper surface. I generally prefer to use the side with the strongest veining

5. Very lightly grease the leaf/petal veiner with cold-cream cleanser. Be careful not to use too much or it will block the finer details and may also create air bubbles in the veiner.

6. Mix another amount of the two compounds as before and press gently on top of the moulded part of the first veiner. Sometimes it is better to add small amounts to very detailed areas and then build up the quantity of compound to form the whole area. Press the compound evenly to pick up all the details. Use a scriber, pin or craft knife to mark the name of the petal/leaf on the wrong side of the compound. Leave to set for 10–20 minutes and then carefully prise the two sections of the veiner apart to make a double-sided veiner. Allow to dry, then rinse to remove any traces of cold-cream cleanser.

Sugar Flowers

Pulled Filler Flower

This technique is often taught in the first lesson of making sugar flowers. In years gone by these pulled flowers were made in their hundreds as filler flowers on cakes. They are quick to make and require very few tools.

MATERIALS
White flowerpaste
Fresh egg white
White vegetable fat (optional)
Cornflour
26- and 28-gauge white wires
White seed-head stamens

EQUIPMENT
Cone modelling tool, pointed dowel, celstick or smooth ceramic tool
Fine sharp scissors
Ceramic silk-veining tool (HP)

1. Take a small piece of white flowerpaste and knead it to warm up the gum in the paste and make it pliable. If the paste is dry add a little fresh egg white. If it is too sticky then add a tiny amount of white vegetable fat. Pinch off a small amount of the paste and form it first into a ball and then, using your finger, work the ball against your palm into a teardrop.

2. Next, hollow out the broad end of the teardrop using the pointed end of a cone modelling tool or with a pointed dowel or celstick or smooth ceramic tool. Remove the tool and then evenly cut the required number of petals using a fine pair of scissors – here five have been created.

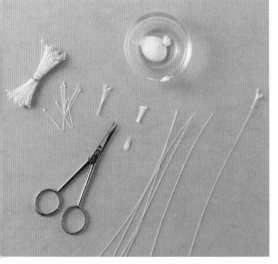

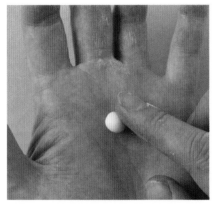

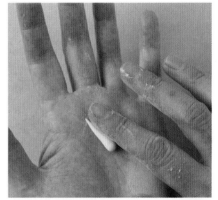

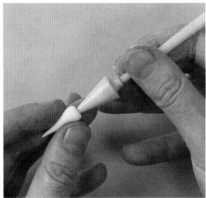

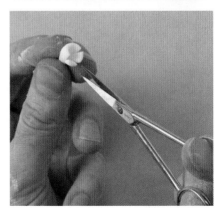

3. Open up the petals and then pinch each between thumb and forefinger into a slightly pointed shape. Flatten each petal to thin out the shape a little.

4. Next, rest the flower against your index finger and using a ceramic silk veining tool broaden, texture and thin out each petal to create a fine frilly effect. You might need to use a little cornflour on your finger to stop the paste from sticking to you.

5. Once all the petals have been frilled remove the flower from your finger and use the pointed end of the smooth ceramic or plastic pointed tool to open up the throat of the flower.

6. Moisten the end of the stamens with fresh egg white and thread through the throat of the flower to embed the stamens into the paste.

7. Use your finger and thumb to roll and thin out the back of the flower creating a slender neck. Pinch off any excess length using your finger and thumb or use a sharp pair of scissors.

8. Finally, give the petals a little more movement. Allow the flower to dry a little and colour as desired.

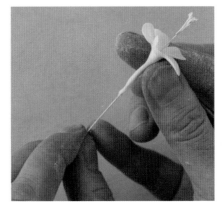
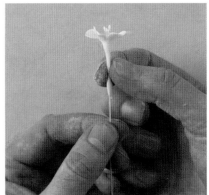

Flamboyant May Flower

The flowers of the flamboyant tree, *Delonix*, are mostly red - however there are white, yellow and orange forms too. The size and length of the stamens differs between varieties.

MATERIALS

22-, 24-, 26- and 28-gauge white wires
Green, white, pale melon and yellow flowerpaste (red for the red flower)
Vine green, foliage green, ruby, sunflower, coral and tangerine petal dusts
White seed-head stamens
Non-toxic craft glue (Pritt)
White vegetable fat
Kitchen paper
Fresh egg white
Cornflour
Nile green floristry tape
Isopropyl alchohol
Edible spray varnish

EQUIPMENT

Wire cutters or sharp florist's scissors
Non-stick board and small rolling pin
Fine paintbrush and flat dusting brush
Large alstroemeria petal cutter or template
Stargazer B petal veiner (SKGI)
Metal ball tool
Firm foam pad
Large hibiscus petal veiner (SKGI)
Ceramic silk-veining tool (HP)
Stencil brush or new toothbrush

PISTIL

1. Cut a half length of 28-gauge white wire using wire cutters or sharp florist's scissors. Take a very small piece of well kneaded pale green flowerpaste and work it onto the wire using your finger and thumb to create a fine coating. Hold the wire firmly with one hand and then work/twiddle the paste firmly with the other. The pistil is about 4 cm (1½ in) long. Start the paste lower on the wire and work it so that it is finer towards the tip. Curve the pistil gently. Dust with vine green petal dust.

STAMENS

2. Take ten white seed-head stamens and line up their tips. Dab a tiny amount of glue at the base of the stamens and squeeze them together. Count to ten and the glue should be set (as long as you haven't put too much glue on!) Prepare several sets of stamens so that by the time you have finished your first set will be dry enough to trim.

3. Glue the stamens to the base of the pistil or use ¼-width nile green floristry tape. Allow the glue to set and then curl the stamens using the side of a pair of scissors.

4. Dilute some ruby petal dust with isopropyl alcohol and paint the length of each stamen a rich red leaving the tips white. In new flowers the tips are more burgundy in colour and in more mature flowers they turn white. Allow to dry and then spray very lightly with edible spray varnish to set the colour.

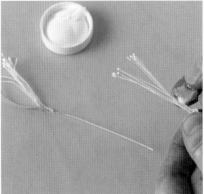

PETALS

5. The method of rolling paste to leave a thick ridge to encase the wire is the method I use for many of the flowers and foliage that I create. Grease the board with white vegetable fat and then remove it using a piece of kitchen paper.

6. Take a piece of flowerpaste and knead it to warm up the gum tragacanth in the paste and to make it pliable and elastic. The gum stops the paste from cracking and crazing. Form the paste into a ball and then into a teardrop and flatten it against the non-stick board.

7. Use a small rolling pin to roll the paste leaving a thick ridge in the centre of one side. I tend to angle the rolling pin on each side of the ridge as I roll so that a tapered effect is created with the broader area being at the base. The exact thickness and length of the ridge will depend upon the type of petal or leaf you are making.

8. Pick up the paste and move it to an area of the non-stick board that is very lightly dusted with cornflour. Use a large alstroemeria petal cutter to cut out the petal. Line up the ridge so that it runs down the middle of the petal. I scrub the cutter slightly against the paste and the board, which encourages the paste to stick in the cutter. Rub your thumb against the outside edge of the cutter to create a clean edge. Remove the petal from the cutter.

9. Next, cut a third length of 26-gauge white wire and moisten the end very slightly with fresh egg white (too much will result in the paper coating coming away from the wire. Insert the wire very gradually into the thick ridge so that it supports about a third to half the length of the petal. Holding the ridge firmly between your finger and thumb and pushing the wire into the ridge with the other hand should prevent the wire piercing the paste.

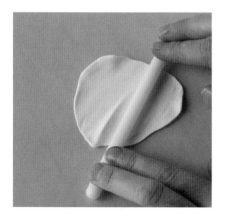

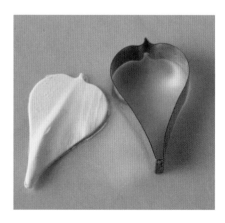

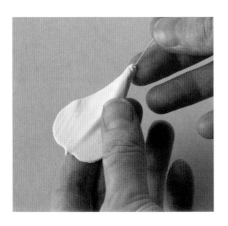 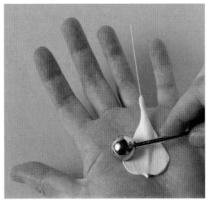 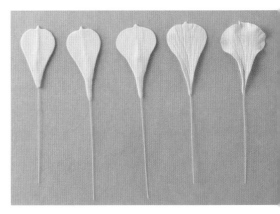

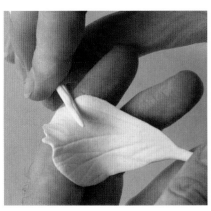  

10. Place the petal against the non-stick board and broaden the top section using a small rolling pin. Next, pick up the petal and place onto the palm of your hand or onto a firm foam pad and use a large metal ball tool to thin and soften the cut edges. Use the ball tool with a rolling action working half on your hand and half on the paste. If you have very hot hands working on the pad might be a better option.

11. To create a realistic texture place the petal into the double-sided hibiscus petal veiner and press the two sides together firmly.

12. Remove the petal from the veiner and rest it against your index finger. Use the ceramic silk-veining tool to frill the edge of the petal at intervals. Be careful not to dig the point of the tool into the petal as this will leave an unsightly mark in the petal.

13. Pinch the petal from behind at the base through to the tip to accentuate the central vein and curve the petal edges back slightly. Repeat the process so that you have one white petal and four pale melon (or red) petals.

COLOURING AND ASSEMBLY

14. Dust the petals while the flowerpaste is still pliable or at a leather-hard stage rather than leaving them to dry, which can make it more difficult to achieve a good depth of colour, as well as being very fragile. Place the petals on kitchen paper and use the powder food colours in layers to create depth and realism. I used a flat dusting brush and tangerine petal dust working heavily from the base and fading out towards the edges of the petal. The backs are dusted too but are slightly paler. Use the flat side of the brush to drag the colour over the raised veins on the back of the petal. Catch the edge of the petal with colour too, bringing it from the edge towards the centre of the petal. Over dust with coral and then a touch of ruby petal dust.

15. Dust the single white petal with a little of the tangerine and coral on the top edge. Dust a patch of sunflower petal dust from the base of the petal on the upper surface. Dilute a small amount of ruby petal dust with isopropyl alcohol. Use a stencil brush or new toothbrush to flick tiny spots and flecks onto the upper surface of the white petal. Add extra spots using a fine paintbrush. Add some fan formation lines from the base of the petal too.

16. While the petals are still pliable tape them around the stamens using ½-width nile green floristry tape. As the paste is still slightly pliable this will enable you to reshape them slightly to create a more realistic shape.

CALYX

17. The calyx is made up from five individual sepals. Cut five 28-gauge white wires using wire cutters or sharp florist's scissors. Take a ball of well-kneaded pale green flowerpaste and work it onto a dry wire leaving the paste broader at the base and forming a fine point at the tip.

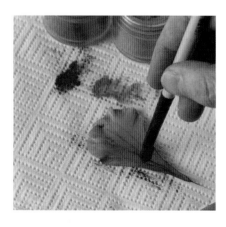

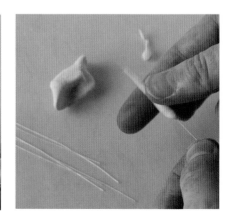

18. Smooth the shape between your palms and then place against the non-stick board and use the flat side of a veiner to flatten the shape. This will make it thinner but also broader. It takes a little practice to get used to knowing just how much the paste will expand. If the shape is not quite as you expected simply trim it using a pair of sharp scissors.

19. Texture the surface using the double-sided stargazer B petal veiner. Place the sepal on your palm and hollow the centre of it using a ball tool. Pinch the paste from the base through to the tip to accentuate the central vein and create a sharper point. Repeat to make five sepals.

20. Dust the inside of each sepal with tangerine and coral (or red for the red variety). Dust the outer surface with vine green and a touch of foliage.

21. Tape the five sepals onto the back of the flower with ½-width floristry tape. Position a sepal inbetween each of the petals. Again, it helps if the paste is still pliable at this stage. Allow the flower to dry and then hold over a jet of steam for a few seconds to 'set' the colour and give a slight shine.

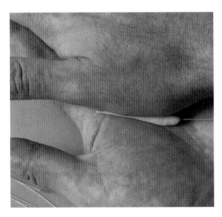

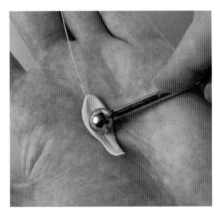

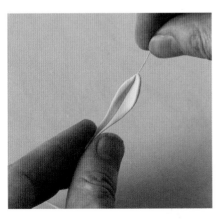

Signature Rose

I teach roses, *Rosa*, more than any other flower. They are the most frequently requested flower among florists and cake decorators for weddings. The instructions described and illustrated here are for the style I use most often. The number of petals differs between varieties and is also determined by the effect you wish to create.

MATERIALS
18-, 26-, 28- and 30-gauge
 white wires
White, red and pale green
 flowerpaste
Fresh egg white
Ruby, kiko, plum, aubergine, foliage
 green, forest green, vine green,
 edelweiss white, daffodil and
 sunflower petal dusts
Nile-green floristry tape
Edible spray varnish or ½ glaze

EQUIPMENT
Fine-nosed pliers
Non-stick board and rolling pin
Rose petal cutters (TT549, 550, 551)
Foam pad
Metal ball tool
Very large rose petal veiner
 (SKGI or FVN)
Cornflour dusting bag
Plastic food bag
Smooth ceramic tool or satay stick
Kitchen paper ring formers
Dusting brushes
Fine sharp scissors
Tape shredder
Curved fine scissors
Large rose leaf cutter (Jem)
Set of three black rose leaf cutters (Jem)
Large briar rose leaf veiner (SKGI)

ROSE CONE CENTRE

1. Use fine-nosed pliers to bend a large open hook in the end of a ½ length (or longer for long-stemmed roses) 18-gauge white wire. Form a ball of well kneaded white flowerpaste into a cone. The cone should be about two-thirds of the length of the smallest rose petal cutter you are using.

2. Moisten the hook with fresh egg white and insert into the rounded base of the cone so that it supports quite a length of the cone. Pinch the paste around the base into the wire to create a strong bond. Reshape the point of the cone, if needed. Allow to dry for as long as possible. Alternatively, bond the hook to the cone. Use a naked flame to heat the hook until it is red hot and then quickly and carefully insert the hook into the cone. The sugar will caramelise and set creating an instant bond. This is especially useful for roses that need to be made in the same day.

3. Colour a large amount of flowerpaste to the required shade. I usually add a touch of vine green, bitter melon or melon for white and other colour roses as this creates a gentle base to which I apply petal dust. When I want a strong pink, orange, yellow or red rose I always colour the paste to a slightly paler shade than I require the finished rose to be.

FIRST LAYER

4. Roll out some of the red flowerpaste fairly thinly using a non-stick rolling pin. Cut out one petal using the smaller of the two rose petal cutters.

5. Place the petal onto your palm or a firm foam pad and then use a metal ball tool to soften the edge. Use the tool half on your hand/pad and half on the petal edge using a rolling action with the tool. Try not to frill the edges – you are simply thinning the edge and softening the raw cut edge.

6. Place the petal into a double-sided rose petal veiner and press firmly to texture the petal. A little cornflour might be needed to dust very lightly into the veiner (especially if it is new) to prevent the paste from sticking.

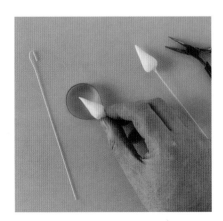
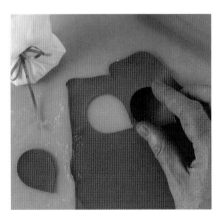
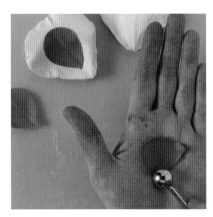

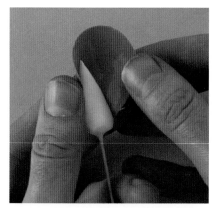
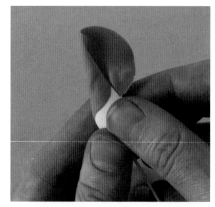
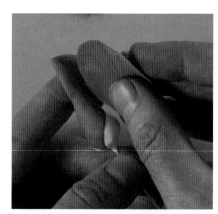

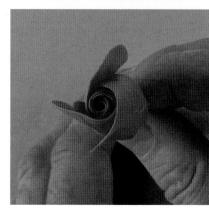

7. Remove the petal from the veiner and moisten (in a 'v' shape) the base of the petal with egg white. Position the petal against the dried cone so that you have enough petal protruding above the tip of the cone. It is important that the tip of the cone is not visible in the centre of the flower when viewed from overhead. Don't worry at this stage about covering up the base of the cone.

8. Tuck/curl the left-hand edge of the petal inward to start to form a tight spiral. Curl the petal around leaving a little of the right-hand edge open so that you can tuck the next petal underneath it.

SECOND LAYER

9. Layers of petals can be created using two petals, though mostly I use three, four or even five petals per layer. Thinly roll out a small amount of kneaded red flowerpaste and cut out three petals using the same size cutter as before. Soften the edges of the three petals and apply the veins. Moisten the base of each petal in a 'v' shape using egg white. Tuck the edge of a petal underneath the loose edge of the first petal that is attached to the cone. Stick down the open edge of the first petal over the new petal.

10. Centre the next petal over the join between the end of the first petal and start of the second. Turn the rose slightly and tuck in the remaining third petal. I tend to keep these petals fairly open to start with so that I can get the height and positioning correct before tightening them around the cone to form a spiral. Leave one of the petal edges slightly open so that it is ready to receive the first petal of the third layer. Some roses have slightly pinched petals – if this is the effect you want, pinch the top petal edges into a slight point using your finger and thumb as you add each layer. Four or five petals can be used to create a rosebud though you should make the cone base a little smaller if you are just creating buds so that the petals cover the whole shape. For a rosebud curl back the edges of the three outer petals and then add a calyx. If you are making a larger rose then keep these three petals fairly tight apart from one petal, which will remain open at the edge ready to receive the first petal of the third layer.

THIRD AND SUBSEQUENT LAYERS

11. The number of layers you use to make a rose depends upon how thin and how tight you make each layer. Roll out more kneaded red flowerpaste and cut out as many sets of three petals as you require using the same size cutter as before. Cover the petals with a food-grade plastic bag or heavy plastic to prevent them from drying out as you work on each layer.

12. Soften the edges of the next three petals and vein the petals using the large double-sided rose petal veiner. Tuck the first petal inside the open edge of the petal from the second layer. Stick both petals in place. Again, add the next petal to cover the join of these last two petals. Add the third petal into the space left behind to form another three-petal spiral. It is important to keep positioning the petals over joins in the previous layer and not to line up the petals directly behind each other. It's also important to keep the petals at roughly the same height or fractionally higher than the previous layer. If you position them too high you will create a rose with a sunken centre.

13. Continue adding the remaining sets of three petals in the same way gradually loosening the petals slightly to create a more open effect. Pinch the top edge of each petal as you add it. Curl the edges slightly as you attach the final layer. You can stop at any stage and add a calyx to create the effect of rosebuds gradually increasing in size, or continue to the next stage to create a half open rose.

HALF ROSE

14. Roll out some more well-kneaded red flowerpaste and cut out three petals using the slightly larger rose petal cutter. Soften and vein the petals as before. This time, start to hollow out the centre of each petal using a large ball tool or by simply rubbing the petal with your thumb.

15. Moisten the base of each petal with fresh egg white, creating a 'v' shape again. Attach the first petal over a join (this time the petals are not tucked underneath). Position the join at the centre of the petal. Pinch the base of the petal on either edge to retain the cupped shape and allowing the rose to 'breathe' a little. Add the second petal next to the first so that it overlaps slightly and then add the third petal in the same way. Use a satay stick, paintbrush handle or smooth ceramic tool or even your finger and thumb to curl back the side edges of each petal (not the top edge as this will create a very flat looking flower). Add pinches to the central top edge too. At this stage you have created a 'half rose'. If the petals are not firm enough to support themselves simply hang them upside down – I often hang my flowers on the kitchen cupboard handles or on a drying stand.

WIRED OUTER PETALS

16. Wired petals give more movement and a less fragile finished flower. Roll out some red flowerpaste, leaving a subtle ridge down the centre. Cut out the petal using the same size rose petal cutter as for the half rose. Bend a small hook in the end of a 26-gauge wire (the hook helps to stop the petals from spinning around). Moisten the hook with fresh egg white and insert it into the base of the thick ridge. Pinch the base of the petal onto the wire to secure it in place. Lightly dust each petal or the veiner with cornflour to prevent the flowerpaste from sticking to the veiner. Soften the edges and vein the petal as before, pressing the veiner firmly to create stronger veins. Remove from the veiner and gently hollow out the centre of the petal using your thumb.

17. Use the smooth ceramic tool, satay stick, paintbrush handle or your finger and thumb to curl back the two side edges.

18. Allow the petal to dry slightly in a cupped shape – I use a kitchen paper ring. Repeat to make eight to ten petals – the number varies with each rose that I make. As the petals start to firm up keep going back to add extra curl to the edges, if required.

COLOURING

19. For pale-coloured roses I tape the wired outer petals onto the half rose and then dust them. For stronger coloured roses I prefer to dust the half rose and the outer petals separately before assembling them. For the dark red roses pictured here I have used a mixture of ruby and kiko petal dusts. Use a flat synthetic fibre brush to scrub the colour onto the outer petals on the back and the front. Some red roses have paler backs so you may dust with white petal dust – the flower pictured was dusted intensely with only the red mixture. Colour the half rose starting at the centre of the flower and working outward. Add extra depth at the centre and on the edges of the petals using aubergine petal dust. If I am working on a pale-coloured rose I always add a 'glow' of colour at the base of each petal on the back and front using a mixture of sunflower, daffodil, white and a vine green petal dust.

ASSEMBLY

20. It is best to tape the wired petals around the half rose while they are still slightly pliable so that you can reshape and manipulate them to form a realistic finished flower. Use ½-width nile green floristry tape to tape the wired outer petals around the half rose. Position the first petal over a join and tape in tightly. Add the next wired petal over a join on the opposite side of the flower. Continue adding the wired petals over joins and opposite each other. Don't be tempted to create a spiral with these outer petals. Take care not to have two petals in complete line with one another.

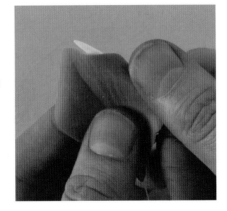 

21. Once the rose is taped together you may need to add extra colour. Allow the rose to dry and then hold it over a jet of steam from a kettle for a few seconds at a time. Take care not to dissolve the rose or burn your fingers. This will help 'set' the colour and also enable you to dust with the strong red petal dusts again to create a more velvety finish.

CALYX-WIRED SEPALS

22. I like to wire each of the calyx sepals. However, if time is tight it is better to add a calyx cut from an all-in-one five-sepalled rose calyx cutter. The wired calyx gives a strong finish to what is generally a very fragile part of a sugar rose and also means the sepals can be longer than those generated using an all-in-one cutter. Cut five lengths of 28- or 30-gauge white wire. Work a ball of pale green flowerpaste onto the wire creating a long, tapered carrot shape – the exact length will depend upon the size of the rose you

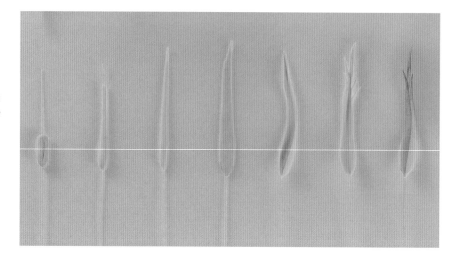

have made and also the variety you are copying as the calyx length varies between varieties. Smooth the shape between your palms and then place against the non-stick board.

23. Use the flat side of one of the double-sided veiners to flatten the shape to thin it out and also 'bulk' out the shape. If the shape is a little distorted simply trim it with a pair of fine sharp scissors. Next, place the shape onto a firm foam pad or the palm of your hand, and soften and hollow out the length of the sepal using a metal ball tool.

24. Pinch the sepal from the base through to the tip and curve the tip back slightly. Use fine sharp curved scissors to cut and create a few fine 'hairs' into the edges of each sepal – the number of cuts varies between varieties – although usually one sepal has no cuts. There are also some varieties of rose that have all five sepals with no cuts/hairs. Flick the hairs back slightly to open them up. If you wish some of the hairs can be flattened using the broad end of the Dresden tool.

COLOURING THE CALYX AND SEPAL

25. Dust each sepal on the outer surface with a mixture of foliage and a touch of forest green petal dust. Add tinges of aubergine mixed with plum or ruby petal dust to the edges and tips of each sepal (this will depend upon the variety you are making). Take care not to break the fine 'hairs'/cuts. Dust the inner part of each sepal using edelweiss petal dust and the brush used for the green mixture on the outer surface. Lightly glaze the outer surface only of each sepal. Allow to dry.

ASSEMBLY

26. Use ½-width nile green floristry tape to tape the five wired sepals onto the back of the rose, positioning each sepal over a join in the petals. Add a ball of pale green flowerpaste at the base of the sepals to represent the ovary. Pinch and squeeze it to create a neat shape. Dust and glaze the ovary to match the sepals.

ROSE LEAVES

27. Rose leaves grow in sets of three or five. I usually create sets of five leaves – one large, two medium and two small. Roll out some mid-green flowerpaste leaving a thick ridge for the wire. Cut out a large leaf using the very large rose leaf cutter. Remove the leaf from the cutter and then insert a moistened 26-gauge wire into the thick ridge to support about half the length of the leaf.

28. Soften the edge of the leaf and then add texture using the double-sided briar rose leaf veiner. Remove the leaf from the veiner and then pinch gently from the base of the leaf through to the tip to accentuate the central vein and give more movement. Repeat to make two smaller leaves and two smaller sizes again. The gauge of wire can be finer the smaller the leaf gets (28- or 30-gauge). Tape each of the leaf stems with ¼-width nile green floristry tape and then tape into a set of five, starting with the large leaf and two medium leaves on each side followed by the two smaller leaves.

COLOURING

29. Dust the edges of each leaf, heavier on one side/edge with a mixture of aubergine and plum or ruby petal dusts mixed together. Use this colour on the upper stem surface too. Dust the upper surface of each leaf in layers from the base fading to the edges with forest green and then heavier with foliage and a touch of vine green. Dust the back of each leaf with white petal dust using the same brush as for the green dusts. Spray lightly with edible spray varnish or glaze with ½-glaze.

Zebrina

Often known as Tradescantia zebrina - named after John Tradescant who was the gardener to King Charles I, this plant originates from Mexico. This wonderful trailing plant is often grown as a houseplant but is also used by florists in bridal bouquets.

MATERIALS
Very pale pink flowerpaste
20-, 22-, 26- and 28-gauge
white wires
Fresh egg white
Foliage green, plum and aubergine
petal dusts
Myrtle bridal satin dust (SK)
Isopropyl alcohol
Edible spray varnish
¼ glaze (see Materials)
Nile green floristry tape

EQUIPMENT
Non-stick board and rolling pin
Sage leaf cutters, cattelya wing petal
cutters or templates
Plain-edge cutting wheel (PME)
Foam pad and metal ball tool
Double-sided stargazer B petal veiner
Small palette
Fine paintbrush and dusting brushes
Tape shredder

1. Roll out some pale pink flowerpaste leaving a thick ridge at the centre for the wire. Cut out a basic leaf shape using one of the cutters or using the template provided and a plain-edge cutting wheel.

2. Insert a 26- or 28-gauge white wire moistened with fresh egg white (the gauge will depend upon the size of the leaf) into the thick ridge to support about half the length of the leaf. Place the leaf onto a firm foam pad or onto your palm and soften the edge of the leaf with a metal ball tool.

3. Place the leaf into the double-sided stargazer B petal veiner to texture the leaf. Remove from the veiner and then place on the foam pad or palm of your hand and add a central vein using the plain-edge cutting wheel followed by a couple of finer lines on each side of the central vein.

4. Pinch the leaf from the base to the tip and curve it very slightly at the tip. Repeat to make leaves in varying sizes. Allow to firm up a little.

COLOURING AND ASSEMBLY

5. There are many varieties of zebrina – here the leaves have been dusted with foliage green on the upper surface. The backs are dusted with plum and aubergine. Catch a little aubergine down the centre of the upper surface too. Allow to dry a little more.

6. Add detail striped markings on each side of the central vein following the curve of the edge of the leaves using a mixture of myrtle bridal satin dust and isopropyl alcohol and a fine paintbrush. Add extra depth if desired using foliage green and a touch of aubergine to paint down the central vein and on the edges of the upper surface. Allow to dry.

7. The leaves are not very shiny but the sugar version benefits from being dipped into a ¼ glaze. I tape them into trailing stems and then spray lightly with edible spray varnish (in a well ventilated area).

8. Tape the leaves onto a 22-gauge wire using ½-width nile green floristry tape. Start with a smaller leaf tightly at the end of the wire and then continue down the stem graduating the leaf size a little as you add them and alternating their position. Bend and curve the main stem slightly. Dust the upper surface of the stem with aubergine petal dust.

Fantasy Flower

Sometimes, a quick and effective filler flower is needed for a cake. This is one of those flowers - although if you add a calyx and alter the leaf it could well be an auricula.

STAMENS

1. Attach six short seed-head stamens onto the end of a 26-gauge white wire using a tiny amount of hi-tack non toxic craft glue. Allow to dry. Dust the tips with sunflower petal dust.

FLOWER

2. Take a ball of well-kneaded pale melon flowerpaste and form it into a slender teardrop. Use your fingers and thumbs to pinch it into a 'hat' shape. Place the brim of the hat against the non-stick board and roll it out using a celstick or smooth ceramic tool.

3. Place the banks rose or auricula cutter over the slender centre and cut into the 'brim'. Scrub the cutter against the board slightly so the paste adheres to the cutter and then pick the whole thing up and rub your thumb against the outer edge of the cutter to create a clean-cut edge.

4. Remove the flower from the cutter and open up the centre using the pointed end of a celstick or smooth ceramic tool. Rest the flower against your finger and thin out each petal, veining it at the same time using a rolling action with the ceramic silk-veining tool. Pinch each petal down the centre to give them central veins and a little more movement.

5. Moisten the base of the stamens with fresh egg white and thread the wire through the centre so that you can only just see the tips of the stamens. Work the back of the flower down the wire to create a slender shape and pinch off any excess paste from the base. Allow to dry. Tape over the stem with ¼-width nile green floristry tape.

COLOURING

6. Dust the petals with a mixture of plum and aubergine petal dust. Dust a mixture of vine green and foliage green onto the base of the flower. Paint a circle of diluted aubergine petal dust around the centre of the flower.

MATERIALS
Seed-head stamens
26-gauge white wire
Hi-tack non toxic craft glue (Impex)
Plum, aubergine, sunflower and vine green and foliage green petal dust
Pale melon-coloured flowerpaste
Fresh egg white
Nile green floristry tape

EQUIPMENT
Non-stick board
Celstick or smooth ceramic tool
Banks rose cutter (TT) or auricula cutter
Ceramic silk-veining tool (HP)
Tape shredder

Clematis

The clematis illustrated here is a simplified form of the flower with a dash of artistic licence. It makes a great filler flower. Although I've used purple flowers, this variety can be green, white, cream, yellow, pink, coral, blue, purple, red and a very dark, almost black, purple. The stamens can vary in colour too.

MATERIALS
White lacemaker's cotton (120 gauge)
22-, 26-, 28- and 30-gauge
    white wires
Nile green floristry tape
Fresh egg white
Vine green, daffodil, white, aubergine,
    African violet, deep purple, and
    foliage petal dusts
Isopropyl alcohol
Edible spray varnish
White and mid-green flowerpaste

EQUIPMENT
Fine sharp scissors
Emery board
Angled tweezers
Non-stick rolling pin and board
Simple leaf cutter (TT) squashed
    or template
Sharp craft knife
Wire cutters or sharp florist's scissors
Firm foam pad
Ball tool
All veined narrow lily veiner (SKGI)
Simple leaf sets (TT)
Dusting brushes
Fine-nosed pliers
Plain-edge cutting wheel (PME)
Clematis leaf veiners

STAMENS

1. Wrap the fine white cotton lacemaker's thread around two fingers (slightly parted) about 20–25 times. Remove from your fingers and twist into a figure of eight shape. Next, fold the shape in half to form a smaller loop.

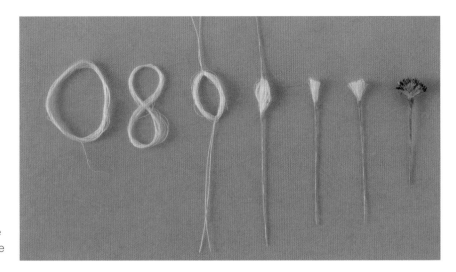

2. Take a 30-gauge white wire and thread it through the centre of the loop and bend it in half over one part of the loop to tighten the wire and hold the thread in place. Tape over the loop of thread and down onto the wire using ¼-width nile green floristry tape. If the loop is large enough you could make two sets of stamens from one loop. Bend another wire opposite the first one and tape as before.

3. Use a pair of sharp fine scissors to cut the thread in half to give two sets of stamens. Trim the threads to make them shorter if required (the length of stamens varies between varieties). Rub the tips of the thread stamens against an emery board to 'fluff' them up a little.

4. Use a pair of angled tweezers dipped in fresh egg white to pinch some of the threads together at the centre. Use the moistened tweezers to curl the outer threads back slightly. The egg white will help stiffen the threads and hold them in place. Allow to dry.

5. Dust the threads with a mixture of vine green, daffodil and white petal dusts. Paint the tips of the stamens with a mixture of aubergine petal dust and isopropyl alcohol. Allow to dry. Spray lightly with edible spray varnish.

PETALS

6. Roll out some well-kneaded white flowerpaste leaving a thick ridge for the wire (a grooved board may be used for this if you prefer). Take a simple leaf cutter and squash to match the template at the back of the book or use the template and a sharp craft knife to cut out the petal.

7. Cut a length of 28-gauge white wire into four using wire cutters or sharp florist's scissors. Moisten the end of a wire with fresh egg white and insert into the broad end of the petal to support about half the length. Pinch the base of the petal onto the wire to secure it in place.

8. Place the petal onto a firm foam pad or onto your palm and soften the edges slightly using a ball tool. Next, place the petal into a double-sided

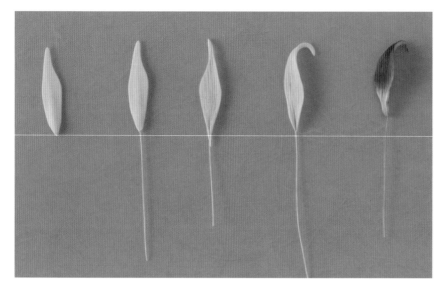

all veined narrow lily petal veiner. Press firmly to texture the petal.

9. Remove from the veiner and pinch the petal from the base through to the tip to give a slight central vein and to curl the petal towards the tip. Repeat to make four petals. Allow to firm up a little before dusting the petals.

COLOURING AND ASSEMBLY

10. Dust the petals while they are still pliable to create an intense colouring. The back of the petals should be paler than the front. Here I have used African violet petal dust with a slight overdusting of deep purple. Leave a small amount of the petal paler at the base. Use the flat of the brush to drag the colour over the raised veins.

11. Mix together vine green and touch of foliage green to add a tinge of colour to the base of the petals on the back and at the tips.

12. While they are still pliable tape the four petals evenly around the thread stamens using ½-width nile green floristry tape. You should now be able to curve the petals a little more to create a more realistic shape. Allow them to dry and then steam gently to set the colour.

BUDS

13. These are quick to make and I often use more of these than flowers on a cake as they offer a quicker way to fill space and continue the colour throughout a cake design. Cut several 26- or 28-gauge white wires into three or four using wire cutters of florists sharp scissors - the gauge of wire will depend upon the size of bud you are making. Tape over each length of wire with ¼-width nile green floristry tape. Next, bend a hook in the end of each wire using fine-nosed pliers.

14. Take a small ball of well kneaded white flowerpaste and form into a chubby cone shape. Moisten a hooked wire with fresh egg white and insert into the base of the cone. Pinch the paste around the base of the bud onto the wire to secure the two together.

15. Divide the surface of the bud into four using a sharp craft knife or plain-edge cutting wheel to represent the four petals. Pinch the tip of the bud into a sharp point. Repeat to make buds in varying sizes.

16. Dust the base of the buds with a light mixture of vine green and foliage green petal

dust. Use African violet to dust the tips of the buds. The smaller buds will be greener. Tape the buds into clusters. Tinge the buds and the upper surface of the stems with a little aubergine petal dust.

LEAVES

17. The leaves occur in sets of three – one large and two slightly smaller ones. Roll out some mid green flowerpaste leaving a thick ridge for the wire.

18. Cut out the leaf using a simple leaf cutters or cut out the leaf freehand using the plain edge cutting wheel. Insert a moistened 24-, 26-, 28- or 30-gauge wire depending upon the size of leaf you are making about half way to give it plenty of support.

19. Place the leaf onto your palm or firm foam pad and soften the edges using a ball tool working half on the edge of the leaf and half on the pad using a rolling action to take away the cut edge. You are not trying to frill the paste.

20. Place into a double-sided clematis leaf veiner. Line up the tip of the leaf and the wire with the central vein in the veiner and press firmly to texture the leaf. Remove from the veiner and pinch from the base through to the tip to accentuate the central vein. Repeat to make more sets of three.

COLOURING AND ASSEMBLY

21. Dust the leaves in layers starting with foliage green. Work the colour from the base fading towards the edges. The backs of the leaves should be paler. Over dust with vine green petal dust. Catch the edges of the leaves gently with aubergine and African violet petal dust mixed together.

22. Tape the leaves into sets of three using ¼-width nile green floristry tape – one large leaf and two smaller leaves at the base on each side.

23. Dust the upper surface of the stems with aubergine petal dust. Spray lightly to glaze them using edible spray varnish or dip them into ½ glaze.

24. Use a 22-gauge wire as the leader for the main trailing stem. Tape one set of small leaves onto the leader wire with ½-width floristry tape. Add two sets of three leaves opposite each other with a group of small buds at the junction. Add leaves and buds of graduating sizes down the stem. Add extra 22-gauge wire if a long length is needed. Gradually introduce clusters of buds with the odd flower followed by groups of flowers. Curve the main stem and dust the upper surface with aubergine petal dust.

Mariposa Lily

The genus of *Calochortus* contains about 70 species often known as mariposa lilies or mariposa tulips. The size, petal shape and colour variations are vast making it an ideal flower to use in creative cake design. Many have tiny hairs at the base of the petals though I often ignore their presence.

STAMENS

1. There are six stamens at the centre of the flower. Small commercial lily stamens could be used to speed up the process of making this flower but it looks prettier if each stamen is handmade. Cut six short lengths of 33-gauge white wire using wire cutters or sharp florists' scissors.

2. Blend a tiny amount of white flowerpaste onto the end of a dry wire to form the anther – there is no need for moisture as this can make such a small piece of sugar very sticky. Work the paste between your finger and thumb to create a point at both ends.

3. Use the plain-edge cutting wheel to mark a line on each side down the length of the anther. Curve the anther slightly if desired (some varieties have curved anthers while other varieties are straight. Repeat to make six stamens.

4. Dust the stamens using a mixture of plum and African violet petal dust and a touch of white.

PISTIL

5. Cut a one-third length of 26-gauge for the pistil. Form a small ball of kneaded white flowerpaste and insert the wire into it. Work the base of the ball down onto the wire using your finger and thumb. Leave the tip of the pistil fairly bulbous. Flatten the top of it with your finger, then use fine-angled tweezers to pinch the pistil from the sides three times.

MATERIALS

26-, 28- and 33-gauge white wires
White flowerpaste
Plum, African violet, vine green, white, sunflower and aubergine petal dusts
Nile green floristry tape
Isopropyl alcohol

EQUIPMENT

Wire cutters or sharp florist's scissors
Plain-edge cutting wheel (PME)
Fine-angled tweezers
Large alstroemeria petal cutter
Non-stick board and rolling pin
Firm foam pad
Ball tool
Stargazer B petal veiner (SKGI)
Ceramic silk-veining tool (HP)
Large ruscus leaf cutter
Sharp craft knife (optional)
Fine paintbrush

6. Colour/dust the pistil using the same colours used for the stamens. Next, tape the six stamens around the pistil using ¼-width nile green floristry tape.

INNER PETALS

7. Roll some kneaded white flowerpaste leaving a tapered thick ridge to insert the wire into. Cut out the petal using the large alstroemeria petal cutter or use the template from the back of the book. Remove the petal from the cutter. Trim a little off the petal base using a pair of sharp scissors to shorten the length.

8. Insert a length of 26-gauge white wire into the thick ridge. Support the ridge as you gently push the wire into about a third to half the length of the petal. Place the petal back on a non-stick board and broaden it slightly across the upper half of the petal using the non-stick rolling pin.

9. Place the petal onto a firm foam pad or on the palm of your hand and use a ball tool to soften the edges, working it half on your hand/pad and half on the edge of the petal. Next, place the petal ridge side down into the double-sided stargazer B petal veiner and press firmly to give the surface a good texture.

10. Remove the petal from the veiner and rest against your index finger. Use the ceramic silk-veining tool to gently frill the upper edge of the petal. Work the tool at intervals along the petal keeping the point of it pointing upward to avoid digging indents into the main section of the petal.

11. Pinch the petal gently from the base through to the tip to create a gentle central vein. Curve the top edge of the petal backward and bend the base of the petal forward slightly. Make three inner petals.

OUTER PETALS

12. Squash the tip of the largest ruscus leaf cutter slightly to create a sharper point. Roll out some white flowerpaste leaving a thick ridge for the wire (you might prefer to use a grooved board for this. Cut out the outer petal using the largest ruscus leaf cutter or use the template from the back of the book and a sharp craft knife.

13. Insert a 28-gauge wire into the thick ridge of the petal to support about half its length. Soften the edge of the petal as for the inner petal and then add texture to it using the double-sided stargazer B petal veiner.

14. Pinch the petal from the base to the tip to create a gentle central vein and a sharp tip to the petal. Curve the petal back from the tip. Make three.

COLOURING

15. Some varieties have a strong yellow patch of colour at the base of the inner petals while others are tinged green. The flower illustrated here was dusted with a mixture of vine green and white at the base on the back and the front. The main body of the petal is dusted with a mixture of plum, African violet and white petal dust. Start dusting from the base of the petal where the green patch of colour ends. Then work from the edge down towards to the base.

16. Dilute some aubergine petal dust with isopropyl alcohol and using a fine paintbrush add some detail markings. An arrowhead formation using a series of smaller brush strokes divides the main flower colour from the pale green patch base. Next, add a series of dots and speckles in varying sizes. Some varieties have very heavy spots while others have very fine detailed spots. There are some varieties without spots. The arrowhead formation often shows through to the back of the petal so, if time allows, you might like to dilute the aubergine colour further and add markings to the back of the flower. This variety also has yellow spots mixed with the aubergine spots – dilute some sunflower yellow petal dust and add some more spotted detail.

17. Use the plum, African violet and white petal dust mixture to dust a streak of colour down the centre of each of the outer petals on the back and the front. Use the vine green and white mixture to catch the edges of the petals.

ASSEMBLY

18. Use ½-width nile green floristry tape to attach the three inner petals around the base of the stamens and pistil. It is good at this stage if the petals are still pliable just in case you need to reshape and curve the petals to create a more realistic effect. Tape the three long narrow outer petals slightly behind the inner petals to fill the gaps between them. Curl and reshape the outer petals, if needed. Dust the base of the flower gently with a little aubergine petal dust. Allow to dry and then steam gently to 'set' the colour and give a slight shine.

Peperomia Leaf

This wonderfully ornate peperomia plant is just one from a diverse family that contains more than 1000 species. The plant is often known as the radiator plant. I have simplified the markings slightly. It makes an ideal foliage for bridal bouquets since it fills space and adds detail and interest at the same time.

1. Roll out a small amount of kneaded pale green flowerpaste leaving a thick ridge for the wire. This leaf is quite fleshy so don't roll the paste too thinly. Cut out the leaf using a peperomia leaf cutter or use the template and a sharp craft knife or plain-edge cutting wheel. Cut a half length of 22-gauge white wire. Moisten the end slightly with fresh egg white and then insert it into the thick ridge of the leaf to support half to two thirds of the length of the leaf.

2. Place the leaf onto a firm foam pad or the palm of your hand and using a large metal ball tool soften the edge, working half on your hand and half on the edge of the leaf. Roll the ball tool firmly rather than rub the edge.

3. Place the leaf into the double-sided extra large clematis leaf veiner lining up the central vein with the tip of the leaf and the wire. If the veiner is new or the flower paste is sticky then dust the leaf or the veiner very lightly prior to veining to prevent it sticking. Remove the leaf from the veiner. Pinch the leaf from behind at the base through to the tip to accentuate the central vein. Allow to firm up a little before colouring by resting it on dimpled foam, ruffled kitchen paper or aluminium foil for support.

4. Tape over the wire a couple of times using ½-width floristry tape. Start the tape a little lower down the stem and then push it up to the base of the leaf.

COLOURING

5. Dust the leaf with myrtle bridal satin dust. Over dust from the base fading toward the edges with a little forest green and then foliage green petal dust.

6. Dilute some foliage green petal dust with isopropyl alcohol and using a fine paintbrush paint in the veins. A few extra veins can be added if there are large gaps. Paint the edge of the leaf with the same colour. Allow to dry.

7. Over dust gently with more foliage green if the painted colour needs calming down. Mix together aubergine, plum and a touch of coral and add a tinge of colour where the wire is inserted into the leaf. Tint the back of the leaf too. Allow to dry and then spray lightly (in a well-ventilated area) with edible spray varnish or dip into a half glaze.

MATERIALS
Pale green flowerpaste
22-gauge white wires
Fresh egg white
Nile green floristry tape
Myrtle bridal satin dust (SK)
Foliage, forest green, plum, aubergine and coral petal dusts
Isopropyl alcohol
Edible spray varnish or ½ glaze

EQUIPMENT
Peperomia leaf cutters or templates
Sharp craft knife or plain-edge cutting wheel (PME)
Large metal ball tool
Extra large clematis leaf veiner (6062a Adv)
Fine paintbrush
Firm foam pad
Kitchen paper or aluminium foil
Tape shredder

Love Berries

The berries of the love plant species make a great quick and effective filler for bridal bouquets and arrangements. The berries of the *Medinilla* species, of which there are 150 worldwide, ripen from white through to pink/purple.

1. Cut several short lengths of 28-gauge white wire. Bend a hook in one end of each using fine-nosed pliers. Tape over each wire, excluding the hook, with ½-width white floristry tape. Use the sides of a pair of scissors to smooth and polish the stems.

2. Next, roll lots of small balls of well-kneaded white flowerpaste. Moisten the hooked end of the wire with fresh egg white and insert into a ball. Pinch the berry onto the wire to secure it in place. The hooked wire should almost pierce through the tip of the berry. Repeat with the remaining balls.

3. Use a pair of fine, sharp scissors to create several small snips in the berry around the hooked-wire area. Repeat with all the berries.

ASSEMBLY AND COLOURING

4. Tape the berries into sets of two and three using ½-width white floristry tape and then tape these small groups onto a 22-gauge white wire to create a panicle (branched cluster) stem.

5. Dust the main stem with a mixture of plum and African violet petal dust. Dust the berries with the same mixture adding a touch of white petal dust to make it a little paler. Dust the snipped area of each berry with aubergine petal dust. Allow to dry and then spray with edible spray varnish in a well-ventilated area.

MATERIALS
22- and 28-gauge white wires
White floristry tape
White flowerpaste
Fresh egg white
Plum, white, African violet and
   aubergine petal dusts
Edible spray varnish

EQUIPMENT
Wire cutters
Fine-nosed pliers
Tape shredder
Fine, sharp scissors
Dusting brushes

Asian Ground Orchid

There are more than 40 species of Asian ground orchid, *Spathoglottis*, distributed from Southern India to China, Malaysia, the Philippines, Indonesia and New Caledonia. The colour variations include white, pink, mauve, red, yellow, apricot and purple. The flower illustrated here is one of the smaller varieties.

MATERIALS
22-, 26-, 28-, 30- and 33-gauge white wires
White flowerpaste
Fresh egg white
White and nile green floristry tape
Sunflower, daffodil, plum, African violet, white and vine green petal dust
Clear alcohol (vodka, kirsch, Cointreau)

EQUIPMENT
Wire cutters or sharp florist's scissors
Spathoglottis orchid cutters (TT824–826)
Non-stick board and rolling pin
Sharp craft knife
Firm foam pad
Small ball tool
Ceramic silk-veining tool (HP)
Cupped Christmas rose petal veiner (SKGI)
Dresden veining tool (J)
Plain-edge cutting wheel (PME)

ANTHER

1. Cut a short length of 33-gauge white wire using wire cutters or sharp florist's scissors. Roll a tiny ball of white flowerpaste and insert the wire into it. Work the paste down the wire to create a slender carrot shape. Press the round tip of the column against the round end of the ceramic silk-veining tool to hollow it out slightly. Give the whole length of the column a gentle curve. Allow to dry. Attach a tiny ball of white paste to the tip of the underside of the column to represent the anther cap. Divide the anther cap into two sections using a sharp craft knife.

LABELLUM/LIP

2. Roll out a small piece of well-kneaded white flowerpaste leaving a thick ridge for a fine wire. Cut out the shape using the oddly shaped labellum/lip cutter from the spathoglottis orchid set. Insert a 30-gauge white wire moistened with egg white into the ridge to support most of the length.

3. Use a small ball tool to soften and hollow out the two 'arms' of the shape. Pinch the length of the shape on the upper surface to create a slight ridge and make it look finer.

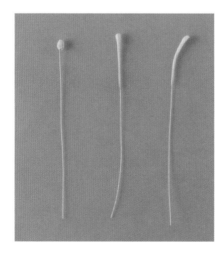
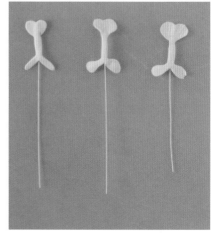

4. Use the ceramic silk-veining tool to texture and thin out the tail part of the shape to make it more fan shaped. Pinch behind the 'arms' of the shape to push them forwards slightly. Bend the length of the labellum a little to add more movement.

5. Attach a tiny, almost heart-shaped piece of yellow flowerpaste to the labellum at the centre of the 'arm' area. Divide the length using a sharp craft knife. This represents the platform.

LATERAL PETALS
6. Roll out some well-kneaded white flowerpaste leaving a thick ridge for the wire. Cut out the petal shape using the wide petal cutter from the set. Insert a moistened 30-gauge wire into the ridge to support about half the length of the petal. Place the petal on a firm foam pad or your palm and soften the edges gently with a ball tool.

7. Place the petal into the double-sided cupped Christmas rose petal veiner and press firmly to texture the petal. Remove the petal from the veiner and pinch gently from the base through to the tip to accentuate a central vein. Repeat to make another lateral petal. Curve both petals back slightly and allow to firm up slightly.

DORSAL AND LATERAL SEPALS
8. These are made in the same way as the lateral petals but this time you need to use the narrower sepal cutter from the set. Curve the lateral sepals (the legs) back and the dorsal (head) forwards.

ASSEMBLY
9. Tape the curved column onto the labellum/lip using ¼-width white floristry tape. The column should curve towards the lip. Add the lateral wide petals onto each side of the throat, again taping tightly with ¼-width white tape. Add the dorsal sepal behind the lateral petals to curve forwards and the two lateral sepals at the base of the flower to curve backwards to complete what almost looks like a figure – a head, two arms and two legs. The back of the orchid has an elongated slender neck. Wrap a sausage of white flowerpaste around the back of the orchid and using your fingers and thumb work the paste down the wire. Pinch off any excess length. Blend the join between the neck and the petals using the broad end of the Dresden tool – sometimes a tiny amount of water or clear alcohol helps to dissolve the sugar slightly to help blend the two together. Curve the neck of the flower.

COLOURING

10. Dust the tiny raised heart-shaped platform in the throat with a mixture of sunflower and daffodil petal dusts. Mix together plum, African violet and white petal dusts to colour the whole of the orchid. Increase the colour at the base and the tips of the petals. Add stronger colouring to the fanned tail of the labellum. Use a touch of vine green at the base of the neck.

BUDS

11. Insert a 26- or 28-gauge white wire into the base of a cone-shaped piece of well-kneaded white flowerpaste. Work the rounded base of the cone between your finger and thumb to create an elongated neck shape. Smooth the neck between your palms and then curve it slightly. Create three sides to the top section of the bud by pressing it firmly between two fingers and a thumb.

12. Mark a single line on each flattened section using the plain-edge cutting wheel. Repeat to make various sized buds. Dust as for the flower.

Gerbera

There are many different varieties of gerbera though the flower described here is the one I use most in cake design. I prefer to wire each petal, which does slow the process a little – but it makes a more realistic flower and is less fragile than a flower made with an all-in-one cutter.

1. Bend a ski-stick hook in the end of a 20-gauge white wire using fine-nosed pliers – start by forming an open hook and then press the hook against the main length of the wire. Now use the pliers and hold the hook across it's centre and bend it back to look like a ski-stick (see Pot Marigold).

2. Roll a ball of well-kneaded white or pink (in this case) flowerpaste. The colour will depend upon the variety — if you are making a flower with a green centre then you will need to use white flowerpaste and then dust the centre later. Moisten the hooked wire and insert into the ball. Pinch the ball around the wire to secure it in place and then flatten the top of the ball and pinch the edges slightly with your finger and thumb.

3. Indent the centre of the shape using the rounded end of a ceramic tool or celstick. Next, use a pair of fine sharp scissors (curved if you have them) to snip lots of tiny hairs around the centre to cover the surface. You might need to re-indent the centre. Allow to dry. At this stage you may decide to colour the centre before adding the fringe.

THE 'FRINGE'

4. Thinly roll out a length of pink flowerpaste. Use the plain-edge cutting wheel to cut a long strip of paste. Use a craft knife or the cutting wheel to make a series of cuts along the top edge of the paste so that it looks like a comb.

5. Use the broad end of the dresden veining tool to indent and soften each of the small cuts. Moisten the base of the 'comb' with fresh egg white and wrap around the sides of the dried centre overlapping the paste if the length of the comb is long. I position the tips of each of the cuts a little higher than the dried centre. Repeat three to four times until the centre is as large as you require. The size of the centre varies between varieties. Flick some of the tiny hair-like petals back slightly. If any of the cuts have blended too much simply go back with fine sharp scissors and add extra snips.

MATERIALS
20-, 28-, and 30-gauge white wires
Pale pink and mid-green flowerpaste
Fresh egg white
Nile green floristry tape
Plum, coral, aubergine, forest and
    foliage green petal dusts
Isopropyl alcohol
White vegetable fat
Nile green floristry tape
Kitchen paper

EQUIPMENT
Fine-nosed pliers
Non-stick board and rolling pin
Ceramic tool or celstick
Fine, sharp curved scissors
Plain-edge cutting wheel (PME) or
    craft knife
Dresden veining tool (Jem)
Large ruscus leaf cutter (TT) squashed
Stargazer B petal veiner (SKGI)
Ball tool and firm foam pad
Tape shredder

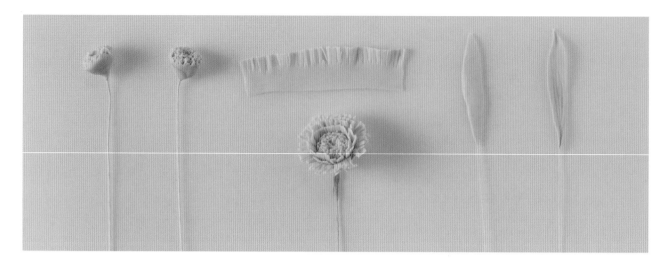

OUTER PETALS

6. The size of the cutter you choose from the ruscus set will depend upon how large you need the flower to be. I have used the largest cutter from the set. One end of the cutter needs to be squashed into a finer point. This fine end will become the base of the petal. Take care not to 'pop' the soldering.

7. Roll out some kneaded pink flowerpaste leaving a thick ridge for the wire. Cut out a petal using the squashed ruscus leaf cutter. Rub your thumb over the outer edge of the paste against the cutter to create a clean edge.

8. Remove the petal from the cutter and insert a moistened 28- or 30-gauge white wire into the thick ridge to support a third to half the length of the petal. The gauge of wire depends upon the size of the petal you make.

9. Place the petal on to a foam pad or the palm of your hand and gently soften the edges of the petal using a ball tool – do not frill them. Texture the petal using the double-sided stargazer B petal veiner. Remove the petal from the veiner and put on the foam pad or palm of your hand and add a few very fine lines down the length using the plain-edge cutting wheel.

10. Gently pinch the petal from the base to the tip. Some gerberas are hollowed out on the back of the petals. At the tip there is often a tiny 'v' shape. If you have time to do this simply use fine sharp scissors to make a cut. Cover the petals with a plastic bag to stop them drying out.

11. You will need to make a lot of petals for this flower – the exact number will depend upon the size of the centre you have made and on the variety. Some gerbera varieties have another layer of petals that are smaller than the outer layer. The flower pictured here has about 50 petals. Make extra in case of breakages.

COLOURING AND ASSEMBLY

12. Dust the fringed hair-like petals around the centre as desired. I used plum with a touch of coral petal dust. The centre of the flower has been painted with a mixture of aubergine petal dust and isopropyl alcohol – take care not to get colour on the fringed petals. Allow the colour to dry a little and then you might find that over dusting with dry aubergine powder hides any streaks.

13. Dust each of the outer petals with the plum and coral petal dust mixture. The underside of each petal should be much paler.

14. While the petals are still slightly pliable tape them around the fringed centre using ½-width nile green floristry tape. Leave a little of the wire showing underneath the centre as this will help to give the base of each of the petals a higher position radiating out around the fringed centre.

15. If extra length or thickness is needed with the stem simply add extra 20-gauge wires and thin strips of absorbent kitchen paper to add bulk taped over with ½-width nile green floristry tape. Use the sides of a pair of scissors to polish the stems and smooth out the joins in the tape.

CALYX

16. Form a ball of kneaded green flowerpaste into a cone. Hollow out the broad end of the cone using the rounded end of a medium celstick. Moisten the centre with fresh egg white and thread the flower stem through the centre. Push it to fit tightly on the back of the flower. Pinch the base and cut off any excess.

17. The calyx is made up from lots of separate fine sepals. This can be created quickly by pressing/embossing the calyx repeatedly with one of the smaller squashed ruscus cutters. Alternatively you can form lot's of fine pointed strands of green flowerpaste. Flatten them and mark a central vein down the inner part of each sepal. Pinch each sepal into place on top of the hollowed out cup shape until you have covered the whole surface. Dust the calyx with a little forest green and over dust heavily with foliage green petal dust. Add the occasional tinge of aubergine, if desired.

Cyclamen Leaf

A popular houseplant that is prized for its unusual uplifting flowerheads. However, the foliage is very decorative and being heart shaped it makes a wonderful addition to sprays and bridal bouquets. The leaves may be plain, variegated or with ornate margins.

MATERIALS
22-, 24-, 26-gauge white wire
White floristry tape
Mid- to dark green flowerpaste
Fresh egg white
Forest, woodland, foliage, edelweiss, plum and aubergine petal dusts
Myrtle bridal satin dust (optional)
Isopropyl alcohol
¼ glaze or edible spray varnish

EQUIPMENT
Wire cutter
Tape shredder or sharp scissors
Non-stick board and rolling pin
Heart-shaped cutters or template
Sharp craft knife
Dresden veining tool (J)
Cyclamen leaf veiners (SKGI) or (Aldv)

1. Cut a length of wire in half – the gauge will depend upon the size of leaf. Cut some white floristry tape into ½ widths. The stalk of the cyclamen is finer close to the leaf and heavy at the base. Tape over the stem several times, each time start the tape a little lower. Smooth over the taped stem and remove the joins left by the tape using the sides of a pair of scissors.

2. Roll out some kneaded mid to dark green flowerpaste leaving a thick ridge for the wire. Cut out the leaves using a heart-shaped cutter or with a sharp craft knife and using the template provided.

3. Moisten the end of the wire with fresh egg white and insert it into the ridge of the leaf to support about two thirds of the length.

4. Place the leaf against the non-stick board and using the broad end of the Dresden veining tool pull out small sections of paste around the edge to give a slightly serrated appearance.

5. Put the leaf into the cyclamen leaf veiner and press firmly to texture the surface. Remove. Pinch from where the wire enters the leaf to the tip to give a central vein. Leave to firm up a little.

COLOURING
6. Dust the upper surface of the leaf with a little forest, woodland and then foliage green petal dust. Dust the back of the leaf with a mixture of plum and aubergine petal dust.

7. Dilute some edelweiss white petal dust with a touch of foliage green and isopropyl alcohol. Use to paint fine veins on the leaf as well as some stippled markings that echo the heart shape of the leaf. If the painted detail is too bright allow to dry and then dust with more foliage green. Dust the stem with foliage and aubergine petal dust. Dip into a ¼ glaze or spray very lightly with edible spray varnish.

Hearts Entwined

Here is one of my favourite succulents, often known as hearts entangled or string of hearts, *Ceropegia woodii*. The variety used here has patterned leaves but other varieties have plain green leaves. I have created just the foliage – the curious tiny flowers are like parachutes that trap insects, encouraging pollination.

1. The leaves could be made with small heart cutters – however, I find this makes them look a little mass-produced and so I prefer to make them using a pulled/freehand method. Cut lots of short lengths of 30- or 33-gauge white wire, depending on the size of leaf you are making. If you can buy 36- or 35-gauge wire, then that is even better for the smallest leaves.

2. Take a small ball of well-kneaded pale green flowerpaste and form it into a cone. Insert a wire moistened with fresh egg white into the broad end of the cone and then place against the non-stick board. Use your fingers to press and squeeze the flowerpaste against the board to form a very naïve heart shape. If you are worried about leaving your fingerprints, then you might prefer to place a plastic food bag over the top prior to forming the shape.

3. Next, hollow out the underside of the leaf using the small ball tool, working on both sides to encourage more of a heart shape. Pinch the leaf from behind to make a very gentle central vein. Repeat to make lots of leaves, pairing them as you work.

ASSEMBLY AND COLOURING

4. I tape the leaves onto a long stem prior to colouring but you might prefer to colour them before taping. Tape two tiny leaves onto the end of a 28-gauge white wire using ¼-width nile green floristry tape. Continue to add the leaves in pairs down the stem, gradually increasing in size as you work. Add extra wire if needed to support the length.

5. Dust the back of each leaf with a mixture of plum and aubergine petal dusts. Catch the upper edges here and there too. The trailing stems also benefit from a light dusting. Use a mixture of foliage and white to dust the upper surface of the leaves. Dilute some foliage with isopropyl alcohol and paint darker green splodges onto the surface of each leaf. Leave to dry and then add some diluted spots of white bridal satin too. Coat with edible spray varnish or steam to set the colour, trying not to make the leaves too shiny.

MATERIALS
28-, 30- and 33-gauge white wires
Pale green flowerpaste
Fresh egg white
Nile green floristry tape
Plum, aubergine, foliage, white and white bridal satin petal dusts
Isopropyl alcohol
Edible spray varnish

EQUIPMENT
Wire cutters
Non-stick board
Plastic food bag
Small ball tool
Tape shredder
Dusting brushes
Fine paintbrush

Flame Lily

Flame lilies, *Gloriosa rothschildiana*, are native to Tropical Africa and India. The flowers can be pale green through to yellow, peach, orange, red and even a deep pinkish-red. The flower is often used in floristry and flower arranging - however, all parts of the plant are toxic, so care must be taken when handling and certainly the fresh flower should not be used on cakes.

MATERIALS
20-, 22-, 24-, 26- and 28-gauge white wires
Pale melon and mid green flowerpaste
Fresh egg white
Nile green floristry tape
Sunflower, daffodil, vine green, foliage, moss and forest green petal dusts
½ glaze or edible spray varnish

EQUIPMENT
Wire cutters
Sharp craft knife (optional)
Plain-edge cutting wheel (PME) Tape shredder
Flame lily cutter or template provided
Stargazer B petal veiner (SKGI)
Smooth ceramic tool (HP) or larg celstick
Plain-edged angled tweezers
Fine-nosed pliers

STAMENS

1. Cut six lengths of 28-gauge white wire. The length (filament) of each stamen is quite fleshy. The length varies between varieties, but generally is not longer than the length of the petal. Work a very small ball of well-kneaded pale melon flowerpaste onto a dry wire. Use your finger and thumb to rub and pull slightly to elongate the paste down to a fine point at the end of the wire. Keep working the paste on the wire removing any excess bulk that might build up at the tip. Smooth the length of the filament and curve slightly. Repeat to make six filaments.

2. To form the anther roll a small sausage of pale melon flowerpaste and attach to the tip of the filament with a tiny amount of fresh egg white. Divide the upper length of the filament using a sharp craft knife or plain-edge cutting wheel. This section can be quite fragile – another option is to bend the tip of the filament wire to form a tiny 'T' bar shape.

PISTIL

3. Twist a length of ¼-width nile green floristry tape back on itself to form a long strand. Cut three short lengths from the strand. Tape the three pieces onto the end of a 26-gauge white wire, using ¼-width nile green tape. Curl the tips of the three end sections back slightly.

4. At the base of the pistil there is an ovary that is divided into three sections. Attach a ball of mid green flowerpaste to the base of the pistil. The length of the pistil can vary too between varieties. Next, form the ball into an oval shape and using a craft knife or plain-edge cutting wheel divide it into three sections. Pinch each section between your finger and thumb to form a slight ridge.

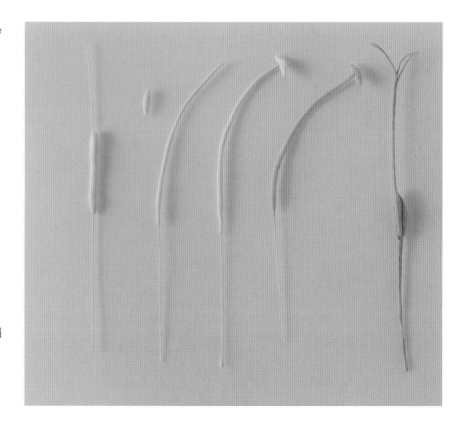

COLOURING AND ASSEMBLY

5. Dust the anthers with a mixture of sunflower and daffodil petal dust. Colour the filaments with vine green petal dust from the base fading towards the anther.

6. Dust the pistil with vine green and moss petal dusts. Glaze with a ½ glaze of spray with edible spray varnish. Allow to dry.

7. Tape the six stamens evenly around the base of the pistil using ½-width nile green floristry tape. If the stamens are too long simply pinch off any excess from the base before taping into place. It helps if the stamens are still fairly pliable at this stage so that you can re-shape them a little, if needed.

PETALS

8. Roll out some well-kneaded pale melon flowerpaste leaving a slender ridge down the centre for the wire. Use a flame lily cutter or the template provided and a sharp craft knife or plain-edge cutting wheel to cut out the petal.

9. Moisten the end of a 26-gauge white wire with fresh egg white and insert gradually in the ridge of the petal, supporting the paste firmly between your finger and thumb to prevent the wire from piercing the paste. Texture the petal using the double-sided stargazer B petal veiner.

10. Next, gently frill the edges of the petal. This can be achieved by either placing the petal against your index finger and rolling at intervals on the edge with the smooth ceramic tool or you may prefer to use the round end of the large celstick. Some varieties are very frilly while others have a fairly smooth edge.

11. Pinch the petal between your finger and thumb from the base through to the tip to create a slight ridge to the back of the petal. Use a pair of plain-edged angled tweezers to pinch a very narrow triangular shape at the base of the petal. Curl the petal back slightly. Repeat to make six petals.

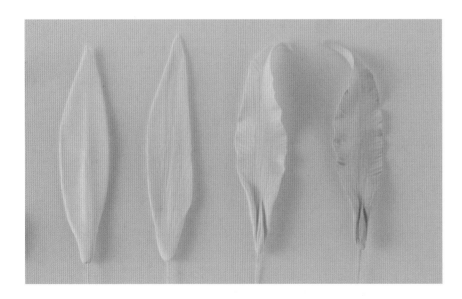

COLOURING AND ASSEMBLY

12. Dust each of the petals with a mixture of daffodil and sunflower petal dust. The older the flower the stronger the colour Dust the triangular shape at the base of each petal with a mixture of moss green and vine green petal dust.

13. Tape a 20-gauge wire onto the stamens and pistil using ½-width nile green floristry tape. Next, tape the petals around the stamens positioning one petal to one stamen. The petals should be slightly pliable at this stage and you should be able to bend the main stem at an acute angle using fine-nosed pliers. Re-shape and curve the petals a little more, if needed. Allow the flower to dry and then steam gently to set the colour.

BUDS

14. Bend an open hook in the end of a length of 24-gauge wire. Tape over the wire with ½-width nile green floristry tape. Next, form a sharp, pointed cone of pale melon flowerpaste and insert the hooked wire, moistened with fresh egg white into the broad base of the shape. Pinch the paste to secure the bud to the wire.

15. Divide the bud into three and then using tweezers pinch a ridge down each section. Finally, give the bud a slight twist at the tip. Dust as for the flower, making the smaller buds green.

LEAVES

16. Roll out some mid green flowerpaste leaving a long thick ridge for the wire. Use the plain-edge cutting wheel or sharp craft knife to cut out a freehand leaf, making sure it tapers into a long slender point. This section of the leaf is usually very long as the plant uses the leaves to wrap around other plants as a climbing mechanism. I generally create the leaves with less length and curl as they can be very fragile.

17. Insert a moistened 22-, 24- or 26-gauge white wire into the thick ridge – the exact gauge will depend upon the size of leaf you are making. Soften the edge of the leaf and then texture lightly using the plain-edge cutting wheel to run a series of fine lines down the leaf and adding a stronger central vein. Pinch the leaf from the base through to the tip and curl the tip almost like a tendril.

COLOURING

18. It is important to colour the leaves while they are still pliable to avoid damaging the fine tips. Use moss, vine green and foliage green petal dust in layers. Curl the tips a little more if needed. Allow to firm up and then spray lightly with edible spray varnish or dip into a ½ glaze.

Pot Marigold

There are many varieties of marigold, *Calendula*, and the size and petal shape vary with some flowers being single and others forming semi-double and double forms. The colour, too, ranges from yellow through to brilliant orange as well as more rusty tones

MATERIALS
24-, 26-, 30- 33-gauge white wires
Pale sunflower and mid green
flowerpaste
Fresh egg white
Nile green floristry tape
Nutkin brown, aubergine, sunflower,
tangerine, coral, vine green,
foliage and petal dust
Isopropyl alcohol

EQUIPMENT
Fine-nosed pliers
Ceramic tool or celstick
Sharp fine scissors
Non-stick board and rolling pin
Ruscus leaf cutter, squashed (TT) or
template provided
Stargazer B petal veiner (SKGI)
Firm foam pad
Wire cutters
Plain-edge cutting wheel (PME)
Ball tool and Dresden veining tool

1. Bend a ski-stick hook in the end of a 24-gauge white wire using fine-nosed pliers. Start by forming an open hook and then press the large hook against the main length of the wire. Now use the pliers and hold the hook across it's centre and bend it back to look like a ski-stick.

2. Roll a ball of well-kneaded pale sunflower flowerpaste. Moisten the hooked wire with fresh egg white and insert into the ball. Pinch the ball around the wire to secure it in place and then flatten the top of the ball and pinch the edges slightly with your finger and thumb.

3. Indent the centre of the shape using the rounded end of a ceramic tool or celstick. Next, use a pair of fine sharp scissors (curved if you have them) to snip lots of tiny hairs around the centre to cover the surface. You might need to re-indent the centre. Allow to dry. At this stage you might decide to colour the centre. I used a mixture of nutkin brown and aubergine petal dust diluted with isopropyl alcohol to paint the textured centre. Allow to dry and then over dust with aubergine petal dust. Set to one side.

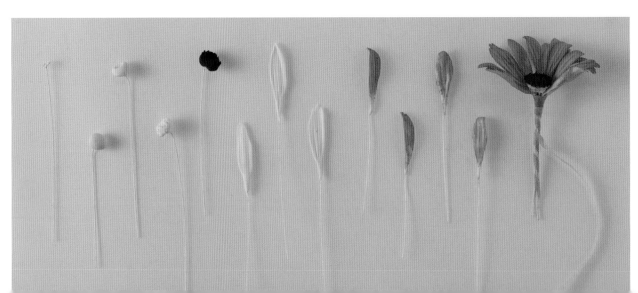

PETALS

4. The shape of marigold petals can vary quite a bit. They can be longer and slimmer than those I have decided to create. Roll out some well-kneaded pale sunflower flowerpaste leaving a thick ridge for the wire.

5. Cut out the petal using a squashed ruscus cutter (see template). Insert a moistened 30- or 33-gauge white wire to support about half the length of the petal. Pinch the base of the petal onto the wire and twiddle it slightly to create a thin base.

6. Put into the double-sided stargazer B petal veiner and press firmly to texture. Remove from the veiner and place in your palm or on a firm foam pad and use the plain-edge cutting wheel to draw three lines down the length of the petal. Turn the petal over and hollow it out very slightly using a small ball tool.

7. Next, cut two tiny 'v'-shaped cuts from the tip of the petal. Repeat the process to make 30–40 petals for each flower.

COLOURING AND ASSEMBLY

8. Dust the base of each petal with sunflower petal dust. Dust the upper surface of each petal heavily with tangerine petal dust. Colour the backs so they are slightly lighter. Add a gentle tinge of coral petal dust to the tips.

9. Tape the petals around the painted centre using ¼-width nile green floristry tape. Leave a little of each wire 'on show' at the base, which will help with the over-all appearance of the face of the flower – if you position them too tightly then the flower will be much smaller and not take as many petals. Trim off any excess bulk created by so many wires using wire cutters.

CALYX

10. Form lots of very fine strands of mid green flowerpaste. Mark a line down each using the fine end of the Dresden veining tool. Attach them to the back of the flower. Dust with vine green and foliage. The calyx is not always essential if the flower is being used in a tight spray.

Renanthera Orchid

There are 15 species of renanthera orchid, sometimes known as flame or fire orchids, found throughout Malaysia, Indonesia, the Philippines and New Guinea. The size of the flower varies between varieties as does the depth of colour.

MATERIALS
Poppy-coloured and white flowerpaste
Poppy paste food colour
22-, 26-, 28- and 30-gauge white wires
Fresh egg white
White and green floristry tape
Coral, ruby, sunflower, white and aubergine petal dust
Isopropyl alcohol

EQUIPMENT
Wire cutters
Smooth ceramic tool (HP)
Sharp craft knife
Non-stick board
Renanthera orchid lip cutter (TT)
Small ball tool
Fine-angled tweezers
Simple leaf cutters (TT) squashed to fit the template provided
Stargazer B petal veiner (SKGI)
Plain-edge cutting wheel

COLUMN

1. Insert a third of a length of 28-gauge wire into a small ball of poppy-coloured flowerpaste and then form it into a cone. Hollow out the underside of the column using the rounded end of the smooth ceramic tool, pressing it against the tool and at the same time forming a slight ridge to the outer surface.EDGE? Allow to dry. Attach a tiny ball of white flowerpaste to the tip of the underside of the column to represent the anther cap. Use a sharp craft knife to split this into two sections.

LIP/LABELLUM

2. Take a small ball of poppy flowerpaste and form it into a cone. Pinch out around the broad base of the cone to turn it into a 'hat' shape. Place the flat side of the 'hat' against the non-stick board and thin out around the central node with the smooth ceramic tool. Place the renanthera orchid lip cutter over the central node and cut out.

3. Soften the side lobes of the shape and hollow the centre of both sections using a small ball tool. Next, use a pair of angled tweezers to pinch two ridges onto the middle pointed section of the lip. Moisten the base of the column with fresh egg white and attach the lip/labellum to the underside. Pinch the two together making sure there is still a space on the back of the column. Curve the pointed section of the lip a little. Allow to dry.

LATERAL PETALS (WING PETALS)

4. Roll out some well-kneaded pale poppy flowerpaste leaving a thick ridge for the wire. Cut out a wing petal using the squashed cutter or use the template provided and a craft knife. Insert a 28-gauge wire into the thick ridge to support about half the length of the petal.

5. Soften the edge of the petal using a ball tool. Do not frill the petal just remove the harsh edge. Place the petal into the double-sided stargazer B petal veiner and press firmly to texture it. Remove from the veiner and pinch the petal backwards from the base through to the tip. Repeat to make a second wing petal (mirror image).

DORSAL SEPAL (HEAD)

6. The dorsal sepal is made in the same way as the wings using the larger squashed simple leaf cutter. Pinch the petal from the base and straighten the shape a little too.

LATERAL SEPALS

7. Repeat the process to cut out two mirror image lateral sepals this time using the largest of the squashed cutters. Insert a 28-gauge wire and texture as before. Curve the petals so that they look bow-legged.

COLOURING AND ASSEMBLY

8. Dust each petal and sepal heavily on the front with coral and then ruby petal dust. Dust the back of each petal/sepal with a mixture of sunflower and white petal dust. Dust the lip/labellum with ruby petal dust.

9. Dilute some ruby petal dust with isopropyl alcohol and paint it on the ridges of the lip/labellum. Add spots to the petals and sepals on the upper surface.

10. Tape the lateral petal as (wings/arms) onto each side of the lip/labellum using ½-width white floristry tape. Add the dorsal sepal between the arms, then add the two lateral sepals so that they maintain their bow-legged appearance. Add some poppy flowerpaste to the stem and add a series of lines using the plain-edge cutting wheel, if you like. (This last step often makes it more difficult to arrange the flowers.)

11. Finally, add a tinge of aubergine mixed with ruby petal dust to the edges of each of the petals/sepals and labellum.

Shivalinga Flower

This is the flower of a fascinating tree often known as the cannonball tree because of its rather large brown fruit that, when dropped from a great height, make a sound like a small explosion.

1. Bend a ski-stick hook in the end of a 22-gauge white wire using fine-nosed pliers (see Pot Marigold). First form an open hook and then press the large hook against the main length of the wire. Now use the pliers and hold the hook across its centre and bend it back to look like a ski-stick.

2. Decide now whether you are making the centre with sugar or cold porcelain. The latter makes it easier to attach the stamens. Form a 2.5 cm (1 in) ball of white flowerpaste and embed the ski-stick hook into the base. Flatten the shape slightly and pinch a point at the centre. Allow to dry.

STAMENS

3. Divide the stamens into groups of 20–30 stamens. Line up their tips and bond them together at the centre by working the glue towards both ends but leaving about 1 cm (3/8 in) unglued. If you are using cold porcelain use a non-toxic hi-tack craft glue which dries quickly and is much easier to control. If you are using flowerpaste then work with the edible glue, which will take longer to dry. Leave to dry.

MATERIALS
22-, 24-, 26- and 28-gauge white wires
Pale melon, mid green and white flowerpaste
Cold porcelain (optional)
Seed-head stamens – 2 or 3 bunches
Nile green floristry tape
Non-toxic craft glue (optional)
Edible glue (optional)
White, vine green, daffodil, sunflower, coral, plum, foliage green, forest, aubergine and edelweiss petal dusts
Fresh egg white
Edible spray varnish or ½ glaze

EQUIPMENT
Fine-nosed pliers
Large rose petal cutter (TT) or template
Sharp craft knife
Large metal ball tool
Very large tea rose petal veiner (SKGI)
Kitchen paper rings (see Equipment)
Standard set of rose petal cutters (TT)
Clay-gun (optional)
Firm foam pad
Smooth ceramic tool/Celstick
Tape shredder
Large sage leaf cutter
Very large mandevilla leaf veiner (SKGI)
Plain-edge cutting wheel (PME)

4. Cut the stamens in half and trim just below the glue line. Use a little more glue and attach the stamen groups around the centre. Squeeze each group to secure them in place. Leave to dry.

5. Dust the centre with a light mixture of white and vine green petal dust. Dust the tips of the stamens with a mixture of daffodil and sunflower petal dust. Use a mixture of coral and plum to dust the length of the stamens.

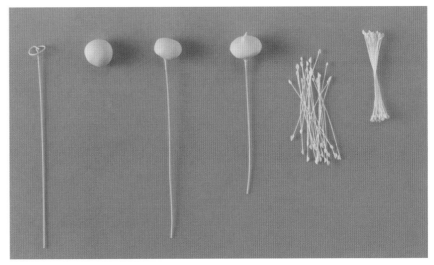

'EYELASH' PETAL

6. Roll out some white flowerpaste but not too thinly, leaving a thick ridge for the wire (this is a fleshy flower). Cut out the petal using a large rose petal cutter or a sharp craft knife and the template at the back of the book. Moisten a 24-gauge white wire with fresh egg white and insert it into the thick ridge to support the whole length of the petal.

7. Soften the edge of the petal with a large ball tool and then place into the very large double-sided tea rose petal veiner to texture the surface of the petal. Remove from the veiner and cup the centre using your thumb or large ball tool. Curve the petal around the wire and then allow to firm up a little resting it in a kitchen paper ring.

8. The 'eyelashes' at the edge of the lip are rolled from flowerpaste one by one and attached to the edge using egg white. This is very time consuming. The other option is to extrude the paste through a clay gun and cut short lengths. Allow to dry a little before colouring.

OUTER PETALS

9. Roll out some well-kneaded pale sunflower flowerpaste – not too thinly and leave a thick ridge for the wire. Cut out a petal using a large rose petal cutter or the template provided.

10. Insert a moistened 26-gauge wire into the ridge to support a third of the petal length. Put in your palm or on a firm foam pad and soften the edge using a large ball tool.

11. Texture the surface using the double-sided very large tea rose petal veiner. Cup the centre of the petal and then curl the side edges back using your fingers or a smooth ceramic tool/celstick. Allow to firm up a little in a kitchen paper ring. Make six petals.

COLOURING AND ASSEMBLY

12. Dust the back of each petal with a mixture of white, sunflower and daffodil petal dust. Use a mixture of coral and plum to dust the upper surface. Dust the 'eyelash' petal with the same mixture adding a little more plum to colour the base of each eyelash. Use sunflower and daffodil petal dust to colour the tips of the eyelashes – taking care as they are very fragile.

13. Use ½-width nile green floristry tape to secure the eyelash petal to the base of the stamen centre. Add the outer petals to the flower in the same way.

CALYX

14. Roll out some mid green flowerpaste leaving a thick ridge. Cut out the sepal using a smaller rose petal cutter. Insert a 28-gauge wire into the thick ridge to support about half the length. Soften the edge and cup the sepal using a large ball tool. Repeat to make six sepals.

15. Dust each sepal with vine green mixed with foliage green petal dust. Tape onto the back of the petals using ½-width nile green floristry tape.

LEAVES

16. Roll out some mid green paste leaving a thick ridge for the wire. Cut out the leaf using a large sage leaf cutter. Insert a moistened 24- or 26-gauge wire into the ridge to support half the length of the leaf.

17. Place the leaf onto your palm or onto a foam pad and soften the edge with a large ball tool. Add veins using the double-sided very large mandevilla leaf veiner. Remove from the veiner and pinch from the base through to the tip to accentuate the central vein.

18. Dust the leaf in layers lightly with forest green. Over dust with foliage green followed by vine green. Add a slightly aubergine tinge to the edge. Allow to dry and then glaze using a ½ glaze or spray lightly with edible spray varnish.

Senecio

Senecio radicans is a wonderful trailing succulent from South Africa. It is often known by its hilarious common name string of bananas. It is related to another trailing succulent that I use quite often on cakes - string of pearls, *Senecio rowleyanus*. There are some varieties with pink-violet stems too. They are effective when sprayed gold or silver for Christmas cakes.

LEAVES

1. Cut several short lengths of 33- or 35-gauge white wire – the finer the better. Form a small ball of well-kneaded pale green flowerpaste into a cone. Insert a wire moistened with fresh egg white into the broad base of the cone.

2. Work the broad base of the cone down onto the wire to create an almost banana shape. Curve the tip slightly.

3. Use a sharp craft knife or plain-edge cutting wheel to mark a single line down the centre of the leaf. Repeat to make more succulent leaves in varying sizes.

ASSEMBLY

4. The leaves may be dusted prior to assembling the trailing stems, but I prefer to tape them up first and then dust them as they are easier to control. Use a 33-gauge 'leader' wire and tape the succulent leaves onto it using ¼-width nile green floristry tape. Start with the smallest leaves leaving a tiny amount of each individual wire on show. Alternate their position down the stem adding extra 33-gauge wire as you work to add more 'strings' of leaves. Curve the central veins uppermost to face the light.

COLOURING

5. Mix together foliage green, a touch of forest green and edelweiss white petal dusts to colour the leaves. Add touches of vine green and a little aubergine here and there too. Spray very lightly with edible spray varnish.

MATERIALS
33- or 35-gauge white wires
Pale green flowerpaste
Fresh egg white
Nile green floristry tape
Foliage, forest, edelweiss white, vine, and aubergine petal dusts.
Edible spray varnish (Fabilo)

EQUIPMENT
Wire cutters
Plain-edge cutting wheel (PME) or sharp craft knife
Fine-nosed pliers
Large dusting brush

Coral

Although coral is time-consuming to make it can make a wonderful fragile addition to a floral arrangement. It is probably best to create and build up the coral over a period of time.

MATERIALS
26-, 33- and 35-gauge white wires
White flowerpaste
White floristry tape
Coral and edelweiss white petal dust
Edible spray varnish (Fabilo)

EQUIPMENT
Wire cutters or sharp florist's scissors
Tape shredder
Small scissors
Fine-nosed pliers
Large dusting brush

1. Use wire cutters or sharp florists' scissors to cut lots of short lengths of 33- or 35-gauge white wires. Take a small ball of well-kneaded white flowerpaste and insert a dry wire into it. Work the paste down the wire using your finger and thumb firmly against the paste to create a fine strand. Curve the length slightly. Repeat to make many strands in varying lengths.

ASSEMBLY AND COLOURING

2. The strands can be dusted before assembly if you prefer, although I often find it easier to colour small items like this when sections of the coral are already assembled. Shred some white floristry tape into quarters using a tape shredder. Use a 26-gauge white wire as a 'leader' wire and tape two or three strands to the end of the wire. Continue adding strands down the stem gradually increasing a little in size as you go.

3. Create several lengths like this in varying sizes and then tape them together into larger pieces of coral. Add stronger wire as you create larger pieces to give extra length and support. Use the sides of a pair of small scissors to polish the white floristry tape and smooth out as many joins as you can. Use fine-nosed pliers to bend and curve the stems a little to give the piece more movement.

4. Dust the coral as desired. The piece illustrated here was dusted with a mixture of coral and edelweiss white petal dust. Spray lightly with edible spray varnish or steam gently to set the colour.

Rangoon Creeper

A beautiful plant from Tropical Asia, also commonly known as drunken sailor because of the way its heavily-laden flower stems sway in the breeze.

1. Use a tiny amount of non-toxic craft glue to bond six short fine stamen tips to the end of a 33-gauge wire. Pinch the stamens in place and hold to secure. Allow to dry. Dust the tips with primrose petal dust.

PETALS

2. Form a tiny cone of apricot flowerpaste and insert a short length of 33- or 35-gauge white wire into it. Work the paste down the wire between your finger and thumb to elongate it. Place the wired shape against the non-stick board and flatten it using the smooth side of the cupped Christmas rose petal veiner. This will thin the petal and form the shape. However, you might need to trim the shape to make the petals even or to tidy the edge. Soften the edge using a ball tool and then place in the double-sided Christmas rose veiner to texture it. Repeat to make five petals.

3. Pinch each petal from the base to the tip, curving slightly to give movement.

COLOURING, ASSEMBLY AND CALYX

4. Dust the upper surface of the petals using varying layers of coral, red and ruby petal dust. Keep the backs very pale. While the petals are still pliable tape them around the stamens using ¼-width white floristry tape. Next, work a small ball of pale green flowerpaste onto the back of the flower to create a long slender neck. Use fine curved scissors to snip five sepals at the top of the neck inbetween each petal. Curve the neck slightly. Dust the calyx with vine green and white mixed together.

BUDS

5. Insert a 33-gauge white wire into the base of a pale green cone-shaped piece of flowerpaste. Work the base of the cone down the wire to create a long slender neck. Curve the neck slightly and then snip fine sepals at the top of the neck as described for the flower.

6. Tint the tip of the bud red and dust the neck with white and vine green.

LEAVES

7. The leaves grow in pairs. Roll out some pale green flowerpaste leaving a ridge for the wire. Cut out the leaves using a squashed simple leaf cutter. Insert a moistened 24-, 26- or 28-gauge wire into each leaf to support about half the length.

MATERIALS
Non-toxic craft glue (Impex)
Fine white stamens
22-, 24-, 26-, 33- and 35-gauge
    white wires
Primrose, coral, red, ruby, vine green,
    white, foliage and aubergine
    petal dusts
Pale apricot and pale green
    flowerpaste
White and nile green floristry tape

EQUIPMENT
Non-stick board
Cupped Christmas rose petal veiner
    (SKGI)
Tape shredder
Ball tool
Fine curved scissors
Plain-edge cutting wheel
Simple leaf cutters (TT) squashed

Ornamental Yam

The genus *Dioscorea* contains about 600 tropical and subtropical herbaceous climbing plants. There are many ornate forms of yam –some with spotted leaves others with highlighted veining in silver, dark green and also pink and red.

1. If you are using the golden wings rose cutters to make this leaf you will need to reshape them to match the yam leaf templates provided. Roll out some mid green flowerpaste leaving a thick ridge for the wire. Cut out the leaf.

2. Insert a 24-, 26- or 28-gauge white wire moistened with fresh egg white into the thick ridge to support about half the length of the leaf. The exact gauge will depend on the size of the leaf you are making.

3. Place the leaf on a firm foam pad or the palm of your hand and soften the edge using a medium metal ball tool. Use a rolling action with the tool, working half on your hand and half on the edge of the leaf. You are only removing the cut edge not trying to frill it.

4. Place the leaf into the double-sided galax leaf veiner and press firmly to add texture. Remove the leaf from the veiner and carefully pinch it from the base through to the tip to accentuate the central vein and give the leaf a sharp point as well as movement. Allow the leaf to firm up a little over crumpled kitchen paper or aluminium foil to help support the leaf in a natural shape.

COLOURING AND ASSEMBLY

5. Dust the leaf while it is still pliable. Use layers of moss, foliage and finally vine green on the upper surface of the leaves. Dust the underside with a mixture of plum and aubergine petal dust fading towards the edges.

6. Add some detail veining using plum and a touch of aubergine petal dust diluted with isopropyl alcohol and a fine paintbrush. Use the textured veins to guide the markings, fading out towards the edges. Allow to dry. Add a tinge of dry aubergine and plum to the base of the leaf where the wire meets the leaf. Spray lightly with edible spray varnish or dip into a ½ glaze.

7. Tape over each leaf stem (about 2.5 cm/1 in) with ½-width nile green floristry tape. Tape the leaves onto a length of 22-gauge wire leaving a little of each leaf stem showing and stagger them down the stem graduating the leaf sizes as you work. Bend each leaf back slightly and curve the main stem too.

MATERIALS
Mid green flowerpaste
22-, 24-, 26- and 28-gauge white wires
Fresh egg white
Moss, foliage, vine, plum and aubergine petal dusts
Isopropyl alcohol
Edible spray varnish or ½ glaze
Nile green floristry tape

EQUIPMENT
Non stick board and rolling pin
Golden wings rose cutters (TT770–775) or template
Firm foam pad
Medium metal ball tool
Galax leaf veiner (SC)
Kitchen paper or aluminium foil
Fine paintbrush

Prayer Plant

There are more than 20 species of *Maranta* from tropical America with varying markings and coloured veins. The common name, prayer plant, is derived from the habit of younger foliage to fold up in the evening. The red veins makes this leaf a wonderful addition to Christmas arrangements.

1. Roll out some well-kneaded pale green flowerpaste, leaving a thick ridge at the centre for the wire. Cut out the leaf using a maranta leaf cutter or using the template provided and a sharp craft knife or plain-edge cutting wheel.

2. Insert a 22- or 24-gauge white wire moistened with fresh egg white into the thick ridge of the leaf to support about half its length. Place the leaf onto a firm foam pad and soften the edge using a large ball tool.

3. Place the leaf into a double-sided maranta or calathea leaf veiner. Press the veiner firmly to create a strong texture. Remove from the veiner and pinch it from the base to the tip to accentuate the central vein. Allow to firm up a little. Tape over the wire with ½-width nile green floristry tape. Add extra 22-gauge white wire if you want to add extra length or strength to the stem.

COLOURING

4. Mix together ruby petal dust with isopropyl alcohol and paint a central vein on the front of the leaf using a fine paintbrush. Add finer side veins in the same way. Allow to dry. Next, dust a line of vine green petal dust between each of the red veins taking care not to get too much green on the red lines.

5. Use a flat dusting brush to work some foliage green petal dust from the edges towards the centre of the leaf, again working inbetween each of the margins created by the red veins. Leave a paler area at the base of each margin where the vine green colouring is. Next, dilute some foliage and forest petal dusts with isopropyl alcohol and paint heavy green markings inbetween the finer red veins. Add this colour to the edge of the leaf to create a border. Leave to dry.

6. Dust the back of the leaf with a mixture of aubergine and plum petal dusts. Over dust areas on the upper surface of the leaf with foliage green petal dust to calm the design a little. Add a tinge of aubergine and plum here and there and to the edges of the leaf on the upper surface. Spray very lightly with edible spray varnish or dip into a ½ glaze.

MATERIALS
Pale green flowerpaste
22- and 24-gauge white wires
Fresh egg white
Nile green floristry tape
Ruby, vine, foliage, forest, plum and aubergine petal dusts
Isopropyl alcohol
Edible spray varnish or ½ glaze

EQUIPMENT
Non-stick rolling pin and board
Maranta leaf cutters or template
Sharp craft knife or plain-edge cutting wheel (PME)
Firm foam pad
Large metal ball tool
Maranta or calathea leaf veiner (SKGI)
Fine paintbrushes
Flat dusting brushes

Cakes and Sprays

Gilded Cupcakes

Cupcakes decorated with swirls of piped buttercream and sprinkled with luxurious edible gold quadrilles are then adorned with unwired sugar pansies, fantasy blossom and gold lace flowers. Lengths of hearts entangled foliage are used to create a frame around the edge of the glass cake stand.

MATERIALS
7 cupcakes
500 g (1 lb 2 oz) buttercream
A jar of edible gold quadrilles
Plum and aubergine petal dusts
Clear alcohol (vodka, kirsch, Cointreau)

EQUIPMENT
Piping bag fitted with a large shell piping tube
Wooden tweezers or chopsticks
Glass cake stand

FLOWERS
5 gold lace flowers
2 burgundy pansy flowers
3 fantasy flowers
4 trailing stems of hearts entangled foliage

1. Fit a large plastic piping bag with a large shell piping tube. Fill the bag with white buttercream and then pipe a swirl of buttercream onto the surface of each cupcake. Start piping at the edge of the cake and work into the centre increasing the pressure a little at the centre.

2. Open the jar of edible gold quadrilles very carefully. Use wooden tweezers or chopsticks to lift and sprinkle some of the tiny squares of gold onto each cupcake. Arrange the cakes on a stand.

FLOWERS
3. Create the unwired pansies, fantasy flowers and gold lace flowers. Tinge the edges of the gold lace flowers with a mixture of plum and aubergine petal dust. Use a little alcohol to dilute some of the mixture to paint the surface of the pansies slightly darker. Allow to dry and then over dust with aubergine petal dust to remove any streaks in the paintwork. Allow to dry.

4. Decorate the cakes using any combination of pansies, gold lace flowers and fantasy flowers.

5. Use the trailing lengths of the hearts entangled foliage to form a frame around the edge of the cake stand.

Mothers' Day Cake

This pretty cake illustrates some very simple design techniques that can be adopted to create a quick and effective cake decoration. Flower cutters are used to emboss the main design and snipped leaves are added using a pair of curved scissors.

MATERIALS

15 cm (6 in) round fruit cake placed on a thin cake board of the same size
25 cm (10 in) round cake drum
450 g (1 lb) white almond paste
450 g (1 lb) pale vine-green sugarpaste
Gold pearl sugar dragées
Small amount of white royal icing
Fine peach and blue ribbon
Broad peach satin ribbon
Cocoa butter
Coral, edelweiss white, vine green, foliage green, sunflower, blue and plum petal dusts
Non-toxic glue stick

EQUIPMENT

Straight-edged sugarpaste smoother
Turntable
Scalloped marzipan crimpers (PME)
Five petal blossom cutter
Fine sharp curved scissors
Small plunger blossom cutters (PME)
No.1, No.2 and No.3 piping tubes
Small stitch wheel (PME)
Smooth ceramic tool or celstick
Scallop marzipan crimpers (PME)
Cup and saucer
Sharp knife
Fine paintbrushes

1. Cover the cake with almond paste and sugarpaste. Cover the cake drum with sugarpaste. Centre the cake on top of the coated cake drum and use the straight-edged sugarpaste smoother to blend the join between the bottom edge of the cake and the drum.

2. Place the cake onto a turntable and use the scalloped marzipan crimpers to pinch/crimp the edge of the freshly coated cake board.

EMBOSS AND SNIP DESIGN

3. Use the larger five-petal blossom cutter to emboss three flowers in a curve on the left-hand side of the cake top. Use the same cutter to emboss sets of three blossom around the coated cake drum and at intervals in the cake side. Use a fine pair of sharp curved scissors to cut sepals and leaves inbetween each of the petals of the embossed flowers.

4. Use the small plunger blossoms to emboss 'filler' flowers into the design around the board and on the cake top. Use No.2 and No.3 piping tubes to emboss a dot in the centre of each of the blossoms and also some fine trailing dots at the design edges. Add stitches using the small stitch wheel.

5. Embed a gold dragée into the centre of each of the large flowers – use a tiny dot of royal icing to hold each one. Use the pointed end of the smooth ceramic tool to add 'eyelet' holes through the design. Leave to dry overnight.

6. Attach a thin band of peach and blue ribbon around the bottom of the cake using tiny dots of royal icing. Attach three ribbon bows at intervals around the base of the cake. Use a non-toxic glue to stick the broad peach satin ribbon to the edge of the cake drum.

PIPING AND COLOURING

7. Fill a piping bag fitted with a No.1 piping tube with a small amount of royal icing. Pipe a fine border around each of the 'eyelet' holes.

8. Fill a cup with just boiled hot water and place a saucer on top. Grate some cocoa butter onto the saucer to melt. Mix in coral and edelweiss white and paint the large flowers. Use a mix of vine green and foliage (plus white) to colour the snipped sepals and leaves. Use blue to colour the small blossoms and sunflower yellow to paint the centre. Add plum to the trailing dots.

Marzipan Rose Cake

A very simple, quick and effective birthday cake decorated with pink marzipan roses to match the very decorative broad rose design ribbon around the base of the cake. This design could be used on a tiered wedding cake - a design like this can be very cost effective and yet still pleasing on the eye.

MATERIALS
900 g (2 lb) white sugarpaste
Bluegrass paste food colour (SK)
18 cm (7 in) round rich fruit cake
placed on a thin cake board of
the same size
750 g (1 lb 10 oz) white
almond paste
27.5cm (11 in) round cake drum
Small amount of royal icing
White pearl sugar dragées
Clear alcohol (kirsch, vodka,
Cointreau) (optional)
Non-toxic glue stick (Pritt)
Wide rose design ribbon
Broad aqua satin ribbon
Foliage, vine green, edelweiss white
and African violet petal dusts
Small amount of cocoa butter

EQUIPMENT
Straight-edged sugarpaste smoother
Cup and saucer
Fine paintbrushes

FLOWERS
1 x full pink marzipan rose (see
following page)
1 half marzipan rose
6 pulled white marzipan pulled
filler flowers
6 marzipan rose leaves

1. Colour the white sugarpaste very lightly with bluegrass paste food colour. Leave the paste to rest and the colour to develop fully before coating the cake; often the depth of colour increases a little.

2. Cover the cake with white almond paste and pale bluegrass sugarpaste. Coat the round cake drum with sugarpaste. Centre the cake on the drum and use the straight-edged sugarpaste smoother to blend the join between the bottom edge of the cake and the coated drum. Leave to dry overnight.

3. Use a small amount of royal icing or sugarpaste softened with clear alcohol to attach the wide rose design ribbon around the bottom edge of the cake. Make sure the seam is at the back of the cake. Use the non-toxic glue stick to adhere the aqua satin ribbon to the edge of the cake drum.

DECORATION

4. Attach the marzipan roses, filler flowers and rose leaves to the top of the cake and cake drum using small amounts of royal icing in place. If the flowers are freshly made they will stick to the sugarpaste without difficulty, but sometimes it's best to be safe. Secure a single white pearl dragée to the centre of each of the white pulled filler flowers.

5. Melt a small amount of cocoa butter on a saucer above a cup of just boiled water. Add some foliage green, a touch of vine green and edelweiss white petal dust to the melted cocoa butter to create a paint. Use a fine paintbrush dipped in the cocoa butter to add trailing vine-like stems to the surface of the cake to soften the edges and add to the design of the marzipan flowers. Add some small pointed leaves. Add more foliage green petal dust to the cocoa butter to add more depth to the leaves.

6. On the opposite side of the saucer mix some African violet and edelweiss white petal dust into an amount of melted cocoa butter. Use a very fine paintbrush to add tiny dotted flower forms at intervals on the painted trailing vine.

Marzipan Rose

Marzipan roses are fairly quick to make and lend instant charm to any cake.
Make them with white almond paste stiffened with a little icing sugar or add
a small amount of flowerpaste for a slightly more flexible medium. Use this technique
to make chocolate paste, sugarpaste and flowerpaste roses.

MATERIALS
White almond paste
Small amount of white flowerpaste
Pink and green paste food colours
Pink petal dust (optional)
Whtite pearl dragées

EQUIPMENT
Food-grade plastic bag
Kitchen cloth or food grade plastic gloves
Sharp knife or scissors
Kitchen paper or aluminium foil
Dusting brushes
Dresden veining tool (optional)
Briar rose leaf veiner (SKGI)

1. Knead the almond paste to soften it and add a small amount of white flowerpaste; the exact amount will depend on how the paste feels to you. I add flowerpaste gradually until it makes the almond paste firm enough to mould a petal easily. It shouldn't overpower the texture and flavour of the almond paste. Add your chosen food paste colour – I used a very pale pink. Wrap the paste in a plastic bag and leave for an hour or so to rest and allow the colour to develop fully – more white almond paste may be needed to lighten the colour.

BASIC CONE CENTRE

2. Take a piece of uncoloured almond paste, knead it and then form it into a smooth ball between your palms. Have a clean, damp cloth to hand as the process can become quite sticky and you will need to keep cleaning your hands. Alternatively, wear food grade plastic gloves.

3. Apply pressure to one side of the ball working the paste between your palms to create an elongated teardrop. Create a 'waistline' towards the base of the teardrop by squeezing the paste between your fingers and thumbs. This will create an elevated platform for the rose petals to wrap around.

PETALS

4. Place a rolled ball of coloured almond paste into a food grade plastic bag. Close the bag, place on the work surface, then press and apply pressure to one side of the ball using your thumb and finger to flatten and thin it and to form the characteristic rounded rose petal shape. The plastic bag makes working with almond paste easy and prevents it sticking to your fingers.

5. Remove the petal from the plastic bag and position it against the teardrop leaving enough petal at the the tip of the cone to curl and spiral around the core and to hide the tip of it. Tuck in the left-hand side of the petal tightly and then continue to spiral the petal around to form a tight, neat spiral. The almond paste will stick to itself quite easily, so there's no need for edible glue or water. At this stage you may stop and use this as a rose bud, in which case you will need to cut off the base of the rose cone with a sharp knife or scissors and then curl back the petal edge slightly. Otherwise you may continue adding more petals.

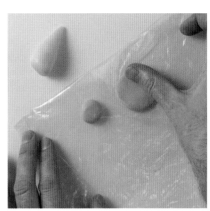
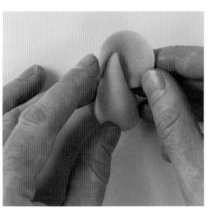
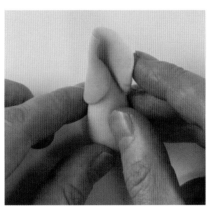
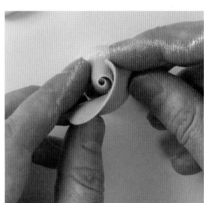

6. Repeat the process to make three more petals. Position the first petal over the join in the first petal, sticking it down on one side of the petal tightly against the cone. Position the remaining two petals at even intervals around the cone to create a spiral. Keep the petals quite open to begin with to allow even spacing. The petal tops should be at the same height as the first petal though they look better if they are very slightly higher.

7. Gradually tighten each petal and curl back the open edges very slightly. I usually pinch the central top edge of each petal slightly too to give a little bit more interest in the shaping. Again you could stop at this stage, curl back the edges and create a more open bud shape. For a fuller rose, you might like to add an equal amount of white almond paste to the coloured paste to lighten it for the next layer, or you can carry on with one depth of colour and simply apply petal dust at the final stages to add more depth at the centre.

8. Roll three more balls of the lighter paste and repeat the process above making the petals slightly larger this time. Thin out the edges of the petals and then add them as before positioning each petal over a join in the previous layer. Allow the petals to open up a little more this time'. Curl back the edges using your fingers to create a more realistic petal effect.

9. Lighten the colour of the almond paste, as before, if you like. Roll 5–8 balls of paste slightly larger than those used on the previous layer. The exact number of petals can vary – it depends upon how blousy you want the flower to be. Repeat the thinning process used previously.

10. Attach the first petal over a join in the previous layer. Pinch the base of the petal to cup it slightly against the rose. Curl back the edges as desired. Place the next petal opposite the first one, again covering a join in the previous layer. Continue adding the remaining petal in opposite pairs and curling back the petal edges as you work. I pinch a central vein in each.

11. Squeeze, or cut off the rose from the basic platform using sharp scissors or a sharp knife. If the rose is very large you might need to support the petals using kitchen paper or aluminium foil until it firms up.

12. The centre of the rose and the edges can be dusted with pink powder, if you like, using a flat dusting brush.

LEAVES

13. The leaves are made using the same technique of thinning the edges in a plastic bag. Use almond paste coloured with green food paste colour. Form a teardrop and place it into the bag. Thin out the edges, which will also create a broader leaf shape. Remove from the bag. Use a Dresden tool to pull out small serrations from the edge of the leaf prior to veining, if you like. Texture the leaf using a briar rose leaf veiner.

14. Pinch the leaf from the base through to the tip to accentuate the central vein. Allow to firm up a little before using in the display.

FILLER FLOWERS

15. These are made from almond paste following the basic instructions for the pulled filler flower. There are unwired. A single white pearl dragée is attached to the centre of each flower.

Filigree Butterfly Cake

This pretty single-tiered birthday cake is decorated with filigree butterflies and pink cosmos flowers and is fairly quick to create using paper-punches that are intended for creative paper craft.

1. Cover the cake with almond paste and sugarpaste. Cover the cake drum with sugarpaste. Position the cake on top of the coated cake drum and use the straight-edged sugarpaste smoother to blend the join between the cake and the board. Allow to dry overnight.

2. Attach a narrow band of lilac satin ribbon to the bottom edge of the cake using a small piped dot of royal icing, or soften a small amount of pale pink sugarpaste with clear alcohol to use as 'glue'. Join the ribbon at the back of the cake. Secure a band of broader lilac ribbon to the edge of the cake drum using a non-toxic glue stick.

TOP AND SIDE DESIGN

3. Cut out and colour the filigree butterflies, fantasy lily shapes, cosmos flowers and foliage.

4. Using a piping bag fitted with a No.1 piping tube and filled with royal icing, secure the pink cosmos flowers and their fine foliage at intervals around the top left-hand edge of the cake and onto the right-hand side of the cake drum. Next, add and secure the purple fantasy lilies, again at intervals to create a balanced design.

5. Add a painted trailing flower and foliage design using foliage and vine green petal dusts mixed with a touch of edelweiss white and clear alcohol to paint the main stem and small leaves. Add extra depth to the leaves by adding more foliage green to the edible paint. Use this mixture to also add detailed veining to the paper-punched cosmos. Use a clean, fine paintbrush and mix together African violet and edelweiss white, again with clear alcohol, to paint a series of fine dotted flowers at intervals on the trailing stem. Use this colour to add some spots to represent stamens for the lilies too. Add extra detail dots to the flowers using diluted bluegrass petal dust mixed with white petal dust.

6. Finally, add the butterflies to the design using more dots of piped royal icing. Add extra detail spots to the centre of the flowers using diluted aubergine. Dilute some gold dust with clear alcohol to make paint and add highlights to the butterfly wings and the flowers too.

MATERIALS

20 cm (8 in) heart-shaped fruit cake placed on a thin cake board of the same size
1 kg (2 lb 2 oz) white almond paste
1.5 kg (3 lb 4 oz) pale pink sugarpaste
12 in (30 cm) heart-shaped cake drum
Broad and narrow lilac satin ribbon
Small amount of royal icing
Clear alcohol (vodka, kirsch, Cointreau)
Non-toxic glue stick (Pritt)
Small amount of royal icing
Foliage and vine green, edelweiss white, African violet, bluegrass and aubergine petal dusts
Edible gold dust (SK)

EQUIPMENT

Straight-edged sugarpaste smoother
Fine paintbrushes
Piping bag fitted with a No.1 piping tube

FLOWERS AND DECORATIONS

7 filigree butterflies
10 cosmos flowers
6 fantasy lily flowers
9 daisy/cosmos leaves

Flowerpaste Paper-punches

I started using paper punches for sugarcraft design several years ago. I found that if flowerpaste is rolled fine enough and allowed to set slightly so that it almost feels like paper then papercraft punches can be used to create very neat designs to use on cakes. I sometimes use rice paper and on other occasions I like to coat the flowerpaste with edible gold or silver leaf before punching out the designs.

MATERIALS

White vegetable fat
White, pink and pale green flowerpaste
Cornflour dusting bag
Plum, bluegrass, aubergine, foliage and vine green, African violet, deep purple and edelweiss white, petal dusts
Whtie and myrtle bridal satin dusts (SK)
Clear alcohol (vodka, kirsch, Cointreau)
Edible gold dust (SK)

EQUIPMENT

Non-stick board and rolling pin
Kitchen paper
Polystyrene dummy cakes
Angled lamp (optional)
Filigree butterfly paper-punch (MS)
Cardboard
Scissors
Cosmos flower paper-punch (MS)
Fine daisy/cosmos leaf (MS)
Palette
Fantasy lily paper-punch (Ww)
Dusting brushes
Fine paintbrushes
Paint palette

BUTTERFLIES

1. Grease the non-stick board with white vegetable fat and remove any excess fat using kitchen paper. Be careful not to leave lots of fat on the board as this will cause greasy spots of colour when the petal dust is applied later.

2. Roll out some well-kneaded white flowerpaste very thinly on the board. You might need to dust the surface using a cornflour-dusting bag. The paste must be rolled evenly otherwise it may block and cause the paper-punch to stick.

3. Place the rolled-out paste onto a polystyrene dummy cake to firm up a little. Polystyrene creates a little heat that helps to dry out the flowerpaste faster. You could use an angled lamp to provide some heat from above. The flowerpaste should be firm but not totally dried out or it will be too brittle to use in the punch. Too soft and it will stick in the paper-punch.

4. Slide the thin sheet of flowerpaste into the filigree butterfly paper-punch and place on a flat work surface. Punch out the butterfly.

5. Cut a rectangular piece of cardboard and fold it into a concertina. Place the cut out butterflies into the indent of the folded cardboard to support their wings as they firm up a little more. You might like to colour the butterflies before allowing them to dry or wait until they are firm.

FLOWERS AND FOLIAGE

6. Use thinly rolled out pink flowerpaste as described above and cut out the cosmos flowers. Use thinly rolled white flowerpaste for the fantasy lilies and pale green flowerpaste for the cosmos/daisy leaves.

COLOURING THE BUTTERFLIES

7. Mix together plum petal dust and white bridal satin dust in a palette. Use a flat dusting brush to catch the edges of the butterfly wings fading toward the centre of each wing section. Dust the backs too. Use bluegrass petal dust and myrtle bridal satin dust to colour the body and reminder of the wings.

8. Dilute some aubergine petal dust with clear alcohol and use a fine paintbrush to paint the butterfly bodies and add detail markings to the tips and edges of the wings. Allow the paint to dry a little and then add some gold highlights using the edible gold dust and a little clear alcohol.

COSMOS FLOWERS AND FOLIAGE

9. Dust the cosmos flowers with plum petal dust applying a heavier coat in the centre and fading towards the edges of the flower. Dilute some plum petal dust with clear alcohol and add fine detail veining to each petal using a very fine paintbrush. Use a little diluted aubergine to add spots at the centre of the flowers to represent the stamen centre. Allow to dry and then use the diluted gold colouring to add highlight dots on top of the aubergine dots.

10. Mix together foliage and vine green petal dust to colour the fine cosmos/daisy leaves working from the base and fading towards the edges. I find it easier to paint details on these leaves once they are attached to the cake as it holds them in place.

FANTASY LILIES

11. Dust the leaf section of the shape with foliage green and the flowers with Arican violet petal dust. Add detail veining using African violet and deep purple diluted with alcohol.

Vintage Florals

Pressed flowers are a delightfully effective way of decorating a cake - especially for the novice cake decorator. This two-tier vintage-looking cake would be great as a birthday cake or perhaps even as a ruby wedding anniversary design.

1. Cover the cakes with almond paste and sugarpaste. Cover the cake drum with sugarpaste. Centre the large cake on the cake drum, then the smaller cake on top. Use the straight-edged sugarpaste smoother to blend the join between the cakes. Leave to dry overnight.

2. Attach a fine ribbon around the base of each cake using royal icing. Tie four ribbon bows. Attach one to the front left-hand side of each cake. Repeat at the back of the cakes. Glue the broad satin ribbon to the cake drum edge.

PRESSED FLOWERS AND FOLIAGE

3. Thinly roll out some well-kneaded pale green flowerpaste. Place it on polystyrene to semi-dry for 30–45 minutes before stamping out several sets of leaves using the ash leaf paper- punch. Dust with foliage green petal dust.

4. To make the pansy, roll out some kneaded white flowerpaste and cut out three large and two smaller rose petals. Remove a small 'v' cut from one of the large petals for the lip petal. Use the ceramic silk-veining tool to broaden and texture the petals, manipulating them into fan-shaped hearts.

5. Overlap and stick the two large petals using fresh egg white. Attach the two smaller petals on each side then the lip petal at the base. Use the broad end of the Dresden tool to embed the lip petal into the centre of the flower. Add a fine 'v'-shaped white paste strand to the flower centre.

6. Take a perspex sugarpaste smoother and 'press' the flower. This will flatten any frills but give a realistic pressed flower effect. Make 3.

COLOURING AND ASSEMBLY

7. Dust the centre of the flower on the lip with a mixture of daffodil and sunflower yellow petal dusts. Use a mixture of plum and aubergine to dust the two large petals and the edges of the other petals. Over dust with aubergine. Use a fine paintbrush to paint some fine lines with black liquid food colour onto the lip and two side petals radiating from the centre of the flower. Highlight the 'eyebrows' with some diluted white petal dust.

8. Paint clear alcohol onto the back of the leaves and stick to the cake. Attach the flower to the the middle of the foliage. Dilute some African violet petal dust with aubergine and paint trailing dotted flowers around the pansies.

MATERIALS
12.5 cm (5 in) and 18 cm (7 in) round fruit cakes placed on thin cake boards of the same size
1.4 kg (3lb 2 oz) white almond paste
1.8 kg (4 lb) champagne sugarpaste
25 cm (10 in) round cake drum
Fine pink border aqua ribbon
Broad pink satin ribbon
Non-toxic craft glue stick (Pritt)
Small amount of royal icing
Small amount of white and pale green flowerpaste
Daffodil, sunflower, plum, aubergine, foliage green, African violet petal dusts
Fresh egg white
Black liquid food colour
Clear alcohol (vodka, kirsch or Cointreau)

EQUIPMENT
Sugarpaste smoothers
Polystyrene dummy
Non-stick board and rolling pin
Ash leaf paper-punch (L-em)
Rose petal cutters (TT) (see template)
Ceramic silk-veining tool (HP)
Dresden tool
Dusting brushes
Fine paintbrushes
Green glass cake stand

Antique Gold Lace Cake

This delicate two-tier antique gold lace wedding cake is very quick to create. The cake and flowers have been decorated in antique gold/ivory but the design would work just as well in pure white.

1. Cover the cakes with almond paste and sugarpaste, then cover the cake drum with sugarpaste, following the instructions in the introduction. Centre the small cake on top of the large cake and blend the join between them using the straight-edged sugarpaste smoother. Attach a fine gold satin ribbon to the bottom edge of each cake using a tiny dot of royal icing or sugarpaste softened with clear alcohol to secure it. Use a non-toxic glue stick to attach the broader gold satin ribbon to the edge of the coated cake drum.

FLORAL LACE DESIGN

2. Thinly roll out some well-kneaded white flowerpaste onto a non-stick board. Cut out the flower shapes using all sizes of petunia blossom cutters, the small plunger blossom cutters and the simple leaf cutters.

3. Dust the floral lace mould lightly with some of the antique gold and gold bridal satin dusts. Place a cut-out petunia blossom over one of the lace flowers in the mould. Press the back of the blossom against the mould to emboss the lace design into the paste and also to pick up some of the gold dust too. Remove from the mould and repeat the process with all the other cut out flowers and leaves.

4. Use the No.1 and No.2 piping tubes to cut out tiny dots around the central area of the flowers to represent the stamens in the design (it's best not to use your best piping tubes for this). Over dust any of areas of the cut-out flowers and leaves with more antique gold dusting powder. Leave to dry a little.

ASSEMBLY

5. Make 4 flowerpaste covered 26-gauge wire sugar curls, following the instructions for the Victorian Frills Cake. Insert a posy pick into the top edge of the top tier and another into the edge of the bottom tier. Fill the picks with a little almond paste and then insert the ends of the wired sugar curls into the pick curving and curling them to create a flowing shape down which the flowers travel. The wires must not pierce the icing or cake.

6. Attach the leaves, blossoms and larger petunia blossoms to the sugar-wired curls using a little royal icing. Fix the smaller plunger blossoms to the ends of each of the sugar curls. Continue to add the flowers and leaves to the sides of the cakes too, overlapping them to create a layered effect. Finally add the sugar dragées to some flower centres securing them with royal icing.

MATERIALS

15 cm (6 in) and 20 cm (8 in) round fruit cakes placed on thin cake boards of the same size
1.4 kg (1lb 2 oz) white almond paste
1.8 kg (3 lb) white sugarpaste
30 cm (12 in) round cake drum
Fine and broad gold satin ribbon
Small amount of royal icing
Clear alcohol (vodka, kirsch or Cointreau)
Non-toxic glue stick (Pritt)
Small amount of white flowerpaste
Gold and antique gold bridal satin dusts
Gold-effect pearl sugar dragées

EQUIPMENT

Straight-edged sugarpaste smoother
Non-stick board and rolling pin
3 sizes of petunia blossom cutters (TT)
5 petal plunger blossom cutters (PME)
Simple leaf cutters
Double-sided floral lace mould
No.1 and No.2 piping tubes
Dusting brushes
26-gauge white wires
Fine posy picks
Piping bags

Butterfly Cupcakes

These delicate floral painted cupcakes work perfectly with my usual floral approach to cake decorating. Here I have combined purple clematis flowers with green and purple butterflies displayed on a very impressive crystal-filled tiered stand. They would be perfect for a small informal wedding or celebration.

MATERIALS
11 cupcakes in silver cases
Apricot glaze
White sugarpaste
Icing sugar
Cocoa butter (SK)
Cocoa powder (optional)
Foliage, vine green, African violet, plum and aubergine petal dust

EQUIPMENT
Non-stick rolling pin
Sugarpaste smoothers
Circle cutter (the size of the cupcake)
Palette knife
Assorted fine paintbrushes
Cup and saucer
Sharp craft knife or scriber
Crystal-filled tiered glass stand

FLOWERS
5 purple clematis flowers
3 clusters of clematis buds
7 sets of clematis foliage
3 fantasy butterflies

1. Wrap a trail of clematis buds and foliage around the tall central part of the crystal-filled glass stand.

2. Place the cupcakes in an informal manner onto the stand. Use the remaining flowers and foliage to simply tuck between the cupcakes to create a balanced overall design.

3. Add the butterflies (see following pages); they are simply threaded alongside the cakes making sure that none of the butterfly wires pierce the cupcakes. Store in a cool place or the design will simply melt away!

Cocoa Painting

Cocoa painting is a very useful technique to use on cakes to create a soft delicate design. The melted cocoa butter can be mixed with cocoa powder or you can mix powder food colours into the cocoa butter to create pretty effects. Cocoa butter is a pure edible vegetable fat that is extracted from the cacao bean. White chocolate is a mixture of cocoa butter, sugar and milk solids. It is a very stable fat containing natural antioxidants that prevent it going rancid. It has a shelf life of 2–5 years.

1. Brush the surface of each cupcake with warmed apricot glaze. Roll out some white sugarpaste thinly using a non-stick rolling pin. Smooth over the surface with a sugarpaste smoother to polish it and create an even finish. Use a circle cutter the same size as the top of the cupcake to cut out a disc for each cake.

2. Fill a cup with just boiled hot water. Place a saucer on top and then grate a small amount of cocoa butter onto it. Allow the cocoa butter to melt and then mix in cocoa powder or petal dusts. Be careful not to allow the cocoa butter to get too warm as the painting medium will be too wet. If the water in the mug starts goes cold then the 'paint' will become quite thick and difficult to work with.

3. On the edge of the saucer mix together African violet and white petal dust with a little of the melted cocoa butter. It is wise to keep some paintbrushes just for painting with fat.

4. The design can be traced and scribed onto the cake first or you can paint freehand; the flower shapes used on the cupcakes are quite easy to execute freestyle. Paint 4 long teardrop petals onto the surface of the cake. Start with the brush at the centre of the flower and taper the strokes into a point. Allow the first layer of colour to set to avoid too much blending/smudging.

5. Mix together vine green and a touch of white petal dust with another small amount of melted cocoa butter and paint in some long pointed leaves and fine flower stems. Allow the colour to set and then add a darker foliage green petal dust to the mixture to add definition to the leaves, colouring heavier on one edge to give the impression of light hitting the surface from the opposite direction. Repeat the process with the flower petals, adding more African violet to the purple mixture and adding lines to represent the veins on the petals.

6. Mix some plum petal dust with a touch of African violet and use to add a series of tiny abstract dotted flowers to the edge off the design. Use aubergine petal dust mixed into a tiny amount of melted cocoa butter to add fine dots to the centre of the clematis flowers to represent the stamens. Leave to set/dry. You could also use a sharp craft knife or scriber to etch fine veins from the petals or leaves, but this will depend upon how dry the sugarpaste coating is.

Fantasy Butterflies

I teach these butterflies often and find they are a very useful addition to cake design. As they are a fantasy piece there are no limitations as to how they are decorated, though they may be painted to represent real butterflies if you prefer. For me these fantasy forms have a much more practical use.

MATERIALS
26-, 28-, 33- and 35-gauge white wires
White flowerpaste
Fresh egg white
Seed-head stamens
Cornflour
White or nile green floristry tape
Vine, African violet, plum, aubergine bluegrass and white petal dusts,
White and myrtle bridal satin dust
Isopropyl alcohol
Hi-tack non-toxic craft glue (optional)
Non-toxic disco glitters (EA) (optional)

EQUIPMENT
Fine-nosed pliers
Craft knife or plain-edge cutting wheel
Non-stick board and rolling pin
Butterfly cutters (Jem) or templates
Metal ball tool
Hibiscus petal veiner (SKGI)
Dusting brushes and fine paintbrushes

1. The body can be made as an all-in-one shape and then divided into sections using a craft knife, or it can be made in three sections and joined together. Use fine-nosed pliers to bend a hook in the end of a 26-gauge white wire. Roll a ball of white flowerpaste for the centre of the body (thorax) and insert the wire moistened with fresh egg white into it. Pinch it firmly to adhere the two together.

2. Next, roll a smaller ball of white flowerpaste for the head. Secure it onto one end of the body with fresh egg white. Divide in half using the craft knife or plain edge-cutting wheel to create two eyes. Form a carrot shape and attach at the other end of the body to represent the abdomen.

3. Use fine-nosed pliers to curl a short length of 33- or 35-gauge wire to represent the tongue (proboscis) and insert it into the head area, through the body and into the tail.

4. Cut one seed-head stamen in half, then trim both halves a little shorter and insert one into each eye to represent the antennae. Leave to dry.

WINGS

5. The butterfly cutters that I like contain the four wing sections in one piece, but this makes it difficult to cut out a wing using the thick ridge method that I prefer, so, I have cut my cutter in half using a large pair of scissors.

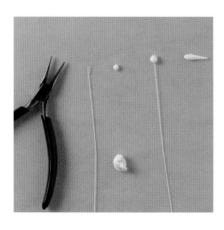 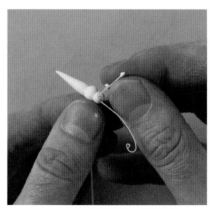 

6. Roll out some well-kneaded white flowerpaste, leaving a fine ridge for the wire. Cut out the larger wing section using the wing cutter. Remove the shape from the cutter and insert a 28-gauge wire moistened with egg white into the thick ridge to support about half the length of the wing.

7. Soften the edge with the metal ball tool and then dust with cornflour to prevent it sticking to the veiner. Place the wing in the double-sided hibiscus petal veiner and press but not so hard that you cut through the paste.

8. Pinch the wing from the base to the tip to give a little movement. Repeat to make the opposite wing plus the two smaller lower wings. Leave to firm a little before assembling and colouring.

ASSEMBLY AND COLOURING

9. Tape the larger forewings to each side of the body using floristry tape. Position and tape the smaller hind wings slightly behind the forewings.

10. Colour the butterflies as desired. I have used a mixture of bluegrass petal dust mixed with myrtle bridal satin to dust the body and the wings, working from the body fading towards the wing edges and then a mixture of plum petal dust and white bridal satin to dust the edge of the wings.

11. Dilute some aubergine petal dust with isopropyl alcohol and paint over the body, antennae and proboscis using a fine paintbrush. Add detail spots and catch the extreme tips with this diluted colour too. Allow to dry.

12. Apply a thin layer of non-toxic craft glue to the tips of the wings and the antennae and dip into disco glitter, if you like. NOTE: although these glitters are non-toxic they are not a food item!, therefore I would only recommend that you use the glitter to decorate items that are not intended to be eaten.

Victorian Frills

Rice paper makes for a very quick and easy way to make cake decorations. Here, this unusual cake has an almost Victorian feel, featuring a combination of a rice paper flower and frills alongside gilded flowerpaste curls. This design would work very well on a tiered wedding cake.

MATERIALS
500 g (1 lb 2 oz) white sugarpaste
Edible gold leaf quad sprinkles
15 cm (6 in) round fruitcake covered in almond paste and placed on a thin cake board of the same size
25 cm (10 in) round cake drum
Fine aqua satin ribbon
Small amount white royal icing
Clear alcohol (vodka, kirsch or Cointreau)
Broad teal velvet ribbon
Non-toxic glue stick
Fine posy pick
Edible gold dust
White floristry tape
White rice wafer paper
Gold dragées
White pearl dragees – various sizes
Non-toxic glue stick
Bluegrass and aubergine petal dust
White bridal satin dust (SK)

EQUIPMENT
Tweezers or chopsticks
Non-stick board and rolling pin
Sugarpaste smoothers
Tape shredder
Piping bag fitted with a No.1 piping tube
Dusting brushes
Fine paintbrush

1. Roll out the sugarpaste and use tweezers or chopsticks to lift out and sprinkle the edible gold leaf quads onto the surface of the paste. Roll over the gold sprinkles with the rolling pin to embed them into the sugarpaste. Cover the cake with the sugarpaste.

2. Repeat the process to cover the cake drum. Centre the cake on the cake drum and blend the join between the cake and the drum using a straight-edged smoother. Leave to dry overnight.

3. Attach a fine band of aqua satin ribbon to the base of the cake using a small dot of piped royal icing or white sugarpaste softened with clear alcohol. Secure a band of teal velvet ribbon to the edge of the cake drum using non-toxic glue stick.

DECORATION

4. Make the rice paper fantasy flower and the fantasy tendrils following the instructions on the following pages. Attach the flower to the top of the cake with royal icing and then push a fine food-grade posy pick into the cake very close to the back of the rice paper flower. Tape together five fantasy tendrils with ½-width white floristry tape and insert them into the posy pick.

5. Cut out and colour more lengths of decorative rice paper using the paper-punch and method described for the outer layer of the flower. Use tiny amounts of white sugarpaste softened with clear alcohol as a glue to attach the rice paper frill, taking care not to dissolve it. Allow to set before adding spots of diluted food colour and edible gold dust as for the fantasy flower.

6. Fill a small bag fitted with a No.1 piping tube with a small amount of white royal icing. Attach the various white and gold dragées at intervals to the cake and the cake drum. Allow to dry. Add tiny painted detail spots to soften the edges of the groups of dragées using a fine paintbrush and the diluted bluegrass and aubergine petal dusts used for the fantasy flower, frill and tendrils.

Rice Paper Fantasy Flower

Rice paper provides a very quick and easy way to decorate cakes. It can be dusted with powder food colour, or painted with melted cocoa butter or clear alcohol mixed with powder colours. Be careful not to get the edible paper too wet or it will dissolve.

MATERIALS
White rice wafer paper
Bluegrass and aubergine petal dust
White bridal satin food colour dust
Edible gold dust
Clear alcohol (vodka, kirsch or Cointreau)
Small amount of flowerpaste

EQUIPMENT
Decorative edge paper-punch (Martha Stewart MS)
Dusting brushes
Fine paintbrush
Dresden tool
Tweezers
Small palette knife

1. Slide the white rice paper into the decorative edge paper-punch and press the lever firmly. There is a guide on the paper-punch to indicate where to move the paper to get it in line to punch/stamp the next section. Punch a length of the rice paper.

2. Dust the cut-out frill as desired. I mixed bluegrass petal dust with white bridal satin food colour dust.

3. To make a flower moisten one end of the rice paper with clear alcohol. Curl the end around and squeeze to create a tight spiral for the centre of the flower. Continue to spiral the length adding a little moisture so it sticks together. Continue to add extra lengths of punched out rice paper to create the size of flower you require.

4. The outer layers of the flower are made in the same way but this time fold the length of the dusted design to create a concertina effect. Attach them to the surface of the cake using a ball of flowerpaste softened with clear alcohol. Form a circle around the paste embedding it using the broad end of the Dresden tool.

5. Use tweezers to position the centre of the flower, embedding it as before.

6. Dilute some bluegrass petal dust with clear alcohol and add spots to each of the petals. Repeat with aubergine petal dust. Add the odd gold spot too using diluted edible gold powder.

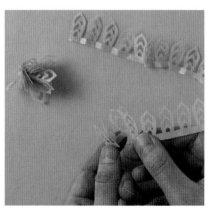

Sugar Curls

These fantasy tendrils (sugar curls) are great fun to create and add an instant touch of grandeur to a cake design or floral spray.

1. Take a small ball of well-kneaded white flowerpaste and blend it onto a length of 26-gauge white wire. Hold the wire firmly at the base with one hand and use your other to work the paste to the tip of the wire to create a fine coating that tapers to a fine point. Pinch off any excess wire.

2. Smooth the length of paste between your palms or against the non-stick board. Repeat to make a few sugar curls. Cover them with a plastic bag if you are worried about them drying out.

3. Hold the tip of the coated wire using fine-nosed pliers. Hold the wire at the base with your other hand. Use the pliers to pull it into an interesting curl.

4. Dust with colour as desired. I have used a mixture of bluegrass and white bridal satin dust applied with a flat dusting brush.

5. Dilute some gold dust with clear alcohol and paint the top sections of each curl/tendril. Add some gold spots too. Dilute some bluegrass petal dust and add more spots then some aubergine spots too. Allow to dry and then spray lightly with edible spray varnish to set the colour.

MATERIALS
White flowerpaste
26-gauge white wire
Bluegrass and aubergine petal dust
White bridal satin dust
Edible gold dust (SKGI)
Clear alcohol (vodka, kirsch or Cointreau)
Edible spray varnish

EQUIPMENT
Non-stick board
Plastic bag
Fine-nosed pliers
Dusting brushes
Fine paintbrushes

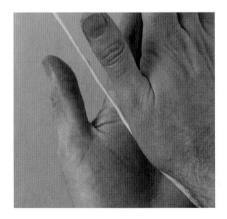
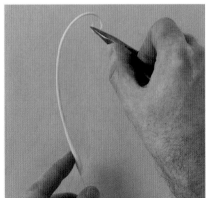
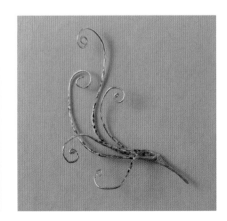

Tropaeolum Stencil Cake

Otherwise known as nasturtiums, *Tropaeolum* are my all-time favourite flower. These cheerful flowers have been created on this three-tier wedding cake using an interior design stencil. The intense, vibrant colours make this a striking cake, but the true creative edge is in the finely detailed painting, which is applied to the final design.

MATERIALS
15, 20 and 25 cm (6, 8 and 10 in) oval fruit cakes placed on thin cake boards of the same shape and size
2.5 kg (4¾ lb) white almond paste
3 kg (5½ lb) white sugarpaste
35 cm (14 in) oval cake drum
Narrow apricot satin ribbon
Broad orange satin ribbon
Tangerine, coral, sunflower, vine green, foliage and aubergine petal dust
Clear alcohol
Non-toxic glue stick (Pritt)

EQUIPMENT
Sugarpaste smoother
Nasturtium stencils (SL)
Synthetic fibre dusting brushes

1. Cover the cakes with almond paste and sugarpaste then cover the cake drum following the instructions in the introduction. Centre the largest cake on top of the coated cake drum and use the straight-edged sugarpaste smoother to create a neat join. Stack the other two cakes on top, centring them carefully and blend the join between the cakes using the smoother. Leave to dry overnight.

2. Attach a narrow band of apricot satin ribbon around the base of each cake using a small amount of royal icing or sugarpaste softened with clear alcohol. Make sure the joins are at the back of each cake. Secure the broader orange ribbon to the edge of the cake drum using the non-toxic glue stick.

NASTURTIUM SIDE DESIGN
3. Use the instructions on the following pages to create several nasturtium flowers, leaves and seed pods. Attach them to the sides of the cakes before they have a chance to dry. Use clear alcohol to secure them. You will need to overlap the leaves and flowers. Add some to the back of the cake too.

Stencilling

Stencilling is a wonderful technique for the cake decorator to add to their repertoire as an almost instant, neat and fairly quick design can be created.

MATERIALS
White vegetable fat
White flowerpaste
Cornflour dusting bag
Tangerine, sunflower, vine green,
coral, red, foliage and aubergine
petal dust
Clear alcohol (Isopropyl, kirsch or
cointreau or vodka etc)

EQUIPMENT
Non-stick board and rolling pin
Kitchen paper
Nasturtium stencil design
Flat, synthetic fibre dusting brushes
Sharp craft knife
Fine paintbrushes
Palette knife

1. Grease your non stick board with white vegetable fat and then clean it off with kitchen paper. This will condition the board and give the flowerpaste a moist surface with which to grip the stencil as well as to collect the colour applied through the stencil.

2. Thinly roll out a piece of well-kneaded white flowerpaste on the non-stick board using a non-stick rolling pin. Dab a little cornflour on the surface of the paste if the rolling pin sticks.

3. Lift the rolled flowerpaste and turn it over. Quickly, put the nasturtium stencil on top of the paste and press it down firmly to create a tight bond.

4. Use a synthetic fibre dusting brush to apply the tangerine petal dust into the petal area. Change to a new brush and dust the nectary with sunflower petal dust.

5. Add a tinge of vine green on top of the nectary, at the tip. Add extra depth to the petals using coral petal dust at the base of each petal fading towards the edges. Use an empty shampoo bottle or photographer's puffer to 'blow' away the excess petal dust.

6. Carefully peel away the stencil from the stencilled design leaving the paste gripping the non-stick board.

7. Use a craft knife to cut around the edges of the design.

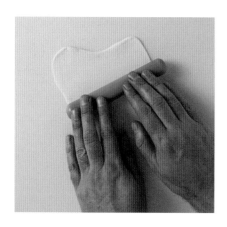

8. Ease and peel the stencilled flower from the board using a palette knife. Turn it over and moisten the back using clear alcohol. Carefully attach the flower to the cake.

9. Repeat to make the yellow flowers using sunflower petal dust. Use more vine green on the nectary.

LEAVES AND SEED PODS

10. The leaves and seed pods are made in the same way using layers of vine green and foliage green to create more depth. Add a tinge of aubergine to the edge of the leaves and seed pods.

ADDED/EXTRA DETAIL

11. Dilute a little coral petal dust with clear alcohol and paint a series of fan formation veins onto each petal of the orange flowers. The yellow flowers have veins painted with a mixture of tangerine and sunflower.

12. Dilute some foliage green with clear alcohol and paint some fine detail veins radiating from the centre of the leaf. Add detail veins to the seed pods and the flower nectaries too.

Flamboyant Christmas Candle Cake

The flame orchid is a rich red flamboyant flower teamed here with ylang-ylang berries to make the perfect decoration for a candle-themed Christmas cake.

MATERIALS
12.5 cm (5 in) round rich fruit cake on a thin cake board of the same size
350 g (12 oz) white almond paste
350 g (12 oz) white sugarpaste
Soft peach ribbon
Clear alcohol (vodka, kirsch or Cointreau)
Small quantity royal icing

EQUIPMENT
Sugarpaste smoother
Nile green floristry tape
Decorative candle holder
Double-side carpet tape (optional)
1 medium posy pick
Fine-nosed pliers

FLOWERS
Festive Flamboyant Spray

1. Place the cake onto a thin cake board of the same size and cover with almond paste and white sugarpaste.

2. Attach a band of pale peach ribbon around the base of the cake using a small amount of sugarpaste softened with clear alcohol, or if you have some to hand, a little royal icing. Allow to dry overnight.

ASSEMBLY
3. Tape together the flowers and foliage following the instructions for the Festive and Flamboyant Spray. Place the cake on top of the candle holder, you might decide to stick it down with double-sided carpet tape.

4. Insert a medium posy pick into the top of the cake and then insert the handle from the spray into it.

5. Use fine-nosed pliers to adjust the position of any of the flowers and foliage that require it.

Festive Flamboyant Spray

Red, green and gold instantly creates a christmas vibe to this vibrant spray of flowers. A red flamboyant flower creates the focal point of the spray accompanied by red renanthera orchids, black ylang-ylang berries and trails of both rustic and gold decorative paper covered wire.

1. Tape any of the flowers, foliage or groups of berries that need extra length or support onto 22-gauge white wires using ¼-width nile green floristry tape.

ASSEMBLY

2. Take a length of rustic green florist's twine and form a loop. Tape a single red flamboyant flower onto the loop using ½-width nile green floristry tape. Add another length of the rustic twine to create a trail. Next, use the gold paper-covered wire to bend three loops around the back of the flower plus three trails. Tape in with ½-width nile green floristry tape. Pinch the three loops of the gold wire into a point to form leaf shapes.

3. Tape the two peperomia leaves behind the flower opposite each other and add the flamboyant buds to trail forwards slightly.

4. Use the sets of clematis leaves to fill in around the spray and use the three stems of senecio foliage to trail and tangle with the rustic and gold wires. Trim off any excess wire as you work with wire cutters or sharp scissors.

5. Add the two renanthera orchids into the spray on each side of the flamboyant flower to create a line of red through the design and finally add the black ylang-ylang berries to run a line of black in the opposite direction through the spray.

6. Use fine-nosed pliers to adjust any of the flowers and foliage. Display in a vase, if desired.

MATERIALS AND EQUIPMENT
22-gauge white wire
Nile green floristry tape
Rustic green florist's twine
Gold decorative paper-covered wire
Fine nosed pliers
Wire cutters or sharp florist's scissors

FLOWERS
1 red flamboyant flower and buds
2 peperomia leaves
8 sets of clematis foliage
3 trailing stems of senecio foliage
2 red renanthera orchids
5 groups of ylang-ylang berries
Decorative vase (optional)

In the Pink

This cheerful pretty pink and silver celebration cake would be great for a small birthday gathering. Pink gerbera flower sprays are complemented by the delicate abstract piped side design on the cake.

MATERIALS
15 cm (6 in) round fruit cake placed on a thin cake board of the same size
350g (12 oz) white almond paste
350 g (12 oz) white sugarpaste
White satin ribbon
Small amount of royal icing
Gooseberry and pink paste food colours
1 x food grade plastic posy pick

EQUIPMENT
20 cm (8 in) silver filigree candle base
Celstick or smooth ceramic tool (HP)
Piping bag fitted with a No.1 piping tube
Fine-nosed pliers

FLOWERS
2 x pink gerbera sprays

1. Place the cake onto a thin board of the same size and cover with almond paste and white sugarpaste Attach a band of white satin ribbon to the bottom edge of the cake using a little royal icing to secure it in place. Centre the cake in the silver filigree candle holder. Allow to dry overnight.

PIPED ROYAL ICED SIDE DESIGN

2. Use the pointed end of a celstick or smooth ceramic tool to create several 'eyelet' holes diagonally to the front and back of the cake.

3. Colour a small amount of royal icing with pale pink food colouring and fill a piping bag fitted with a No.1 piping tube. Next, pipe around the edge of each of the eyelet holes followed by a series of pink tapered lines to represent an abstract gerbera flower shape. Fill another small piping bag fitted with a No.1 piping tube with gooseberry royal icing. Pipe a trailing stem followed by a few small leaves.

4. Now, revert back to the piping bag with pink royal icing to add a series of dots to soften the edge of the design.

5. Construct the two sprays following the instructions for the pink gerbera sprays. Insert a food grade plastic posy pick into the top of the cake and position the handle of one of the gerbera sprays into it. Use fine-nosed pliers to reposition any of the leaves or decorative paper covered wire trails. Add the second gerbera spray to the base of the cake to rest on the edge of the silver filigree candle base.

Pink Gerbera Spray

A single gerbera flower is immediately eye-catching . Silver and bright pink decorative paper-covered wires are used here to add length and continue the colour theme throughout the length of the spray.

1. Use 22-gauge wire and ½-width nile green floristry tape to add extra length or strength to any of the flower and foliage stems, if needed.

ASSEMBLY

2. Use lengths of bright pink and silver decorative paper-covered wire to add several loops behind a single gerbera flower. Grip the wires firmly against the flower stem with your fingers and then tape them into place using ½-width nile green floristry tape. Add a few trails to create the total length of the spray. Use fine-nosed pliers to curl the ends.

3. Add the cyclamen foliage to frame the gerbera flower taping the leaves with ½-width nile green floristry tape. Use wire cutters or sharp florist's scissors to trim any excess wire from the leaves.

4. Finally, add trails of senecio foliage alongside the long trails of decorative paper-covered wire. Add extra lengths of senecio to follow the loops of wire at the top of the spray. Repeat the process to make a second spray in the same way. Display in a small green vase.

MATERIALS AND EQUIPMENT
22-gauge white wire
Nile green floristry tape
Bright pink and silver decorative paper
  covered wire
Fine-nosed pliers
Wire cutters or sharp florist's scissors
Small green vase

FLOWERS AND FOLIAGE
2 pink gerbera flowers
12 cyclamen leaves
8 trailing stems of senecio foliage

All That Glitters

This stunning two-tier golden wedding anniversary cake would make an exotic wedding cake too. Golden yellow flame lilies and black ylang-ylang berries are combined with trails of gold paper-covered wires and a gilded royal-iced piped and painted butterfly side design.

MATERIALS
13 cm (5 in) and 20 cm (8 in) round fruit cakes placed on thin cake boards of the same size
1 kg (2 lb) white almond paste
1.4 kg (3 lb) white sugarpaste
30 cm (12 in) round cake drum
Wide and narrow soft gold satin ribbon
Non-toxic glue stick (Pritt)
Small amount of royal icing in a piping bag fitted with a No.1 piping tube
Edible gold powder food colour
Clear alcohol (kirsch or Cointreau)
Small amount of mid green flowerpaste
Foliage and vine green, daffodil, white and sunflower yellow petal dust
Edible spray varnish
Nile green floristry tape

EQUIPMENT
Straight-edged sugarpaste smoother
Template of butterfly (see back of book)
Tracing paper or greaseproof paper and pencil
Fine scriber, pin or a ballpoint pen that has run out of ink
1 medium and 1 fine food grade plastic posy pick
Antique gold-effect shallow candle holder
Fine paintbrushes and palette

FLOWERS
2 golden flame lily sprays

1. Cover both cakes with almond paste and white sugarpaste as described in the introduction. Cover the large cake drum with white sugarpaste.

2. Centre the large coated cake on top of the cake drum and use the straight-edged sugarpaste smoother to blend the join between the base of the cake and the drum. Centre the smaller cake on the base tier and blend the join as before. Leave to dry for a few days.

3. Attach a narrow band of soft gold satin ribbon around the base of both cakes using tiny dots of royal icing. Use the non-toxic glue stick to attach the wide soft gold satin ribbon to the edge of the cake drum.

BUTTERFLY SIDE DESIGN

4. The butterflies are piped freehand onto the side of the cakes using a piping bag fitted with a No.1 piping tube and then filled with a little white royal icing. You might prefer to scribe the design into the icing using the template from the back of the book traced onto tracing paper or greaseproof paper. Pipe the butterfly wings first, almost 'scratch' the design to keep it fairly fine. Next, fill the butterfly body applying more pressure this time with the bag. Add two fine dots to represent the antennae. Repeat to pipe several butterflies at the front and at the back of both cakes. Allow to dry.

5. Dilute some edible gold powder food colour with clear alcohol and paint over the butterfly bodies using a fine paintbrush. Add a series of fine trailing dots behind each butterfly using the gold paint too.

6. Next, dilute some sunflower, daffodil and a touch of white petal dust to add some detail markings to the wings. Repeat the process with a mixture of vine green and foliage green to add darker markings to the design. Leave to dry.

ASSEMBLY

7. Insert the larger golden flame lily spray into the medium-sized food-grade plastic posy pick inserted into the top tier of the cake. Use the finer posy pick to hold the smaller spray at the base of the larger cake.

8. Display the cake elevated onto an antique gold-effect shallow candle holder or similar. Use fine-nosed pliers to bend and curve any of the flower and foliage stems to create an attractive overall display.

Golden Flame Lily Spray

Flame lilies can be very fragile when made in sugar and so it's important to give them plenty of space to spread out. Here, I have combined them very simply with black ylang-ylang berries and gold paper-covered wire.

1. Add extra length or strength to the flame lily or the ylang-ylang berries if required by taping 22-gauge white wire onto their main stems using ½-width nile green floristry tape.

ASSEMBLY

2. Take a long stem of the flame lily, buds and foliage and tape two large yellow flame lily flowers at the base using ½-width nile green floristry tape.

3. Add five sets of ylang-ylang berries to fill the space on each side of the lilies. Trim off any excess wire with sharp floristry scissors or wire cutters.

4. Use several flame lily leaves to frame the base of the display radiating out from the main stem. Tape them tightly using ½-width nile green floristry tape so that the wires are hidden. Take a length of gold decorative paper-covered wire and hold one end just underneath the flame lily leaves and form three loops spaced evenly around the base of the spray. Trim off the excess length and tape into place with ½-width floristry tape. Add three long trails of gold paper-covered wire to the left-hand side of the spray. Use wire cutters to trim their lengths and then curl the ends using fine-nosed pliers.

SMALLER SPRAY

5. Tape a large yellow flame lily onto a stem of flame lily buds and foliage using ½-width floristry tape. Add three sets of ylang-ylang berries evenly spaced to the right-hand side of the main flower.

6. Add extra flame lily leaves to frame the base of the spray and then add loops and trails of gold paper-covered wire, but not as much length as for the larger spray.

7. Place the larger spray into a slender-neck vase and the smaller spray simply rests against the base at the vase.

MATERIALS AND EQUIPMENT
22-gauge white wire
Nile green floristry tape
Wire cutters or sharp floristry scissors
Gold decorative paper-covered wire (APOC)
Fine-nosed pliers
Metallic-effect slender-neck black vase

FLOWERS AND FOLIAGE
3 yellow flame lilies and their buds and foliage
7 sets of ylang-ylang berries

August Wedding

A rich, luxurious combination of almost velvet-textured red roses and purple clematis adorn this romantic three-tier wedding cake. The side design of sugar pearl dragees and edible silver leaf cutout foliage enhances the overall display.

MATERIALS

13 cm (5 in), 20 cm (8 in) and 28 cm (11 in) round rich fruit cakes placed on thin cake boards of the same size
3 kg (6 lb) white almond paste
Apricot glaze
5 kg (10 lb) champagne sugarpaste
40cm (16in) round cake drum
Red velvet ribbon to trim the cake drum
Non-toxic glue stick (Pritt)
Ivory ribbon to trim the cakes
Small amount of royal icing in a piping bag fitted with a No.1 piping tube
Edible silver leaf sheets
Small amount of flowerpaste
Clear alcohol (kirsch or Cointreau)
Large pearl dragées

EQUIPMENT

Straight-edged sugarpaste smoother
Make-up sponge
Non-stick board and rolling pin
Jasmine leaf paper punch
2 posy picks

FLOWERS

2 red rose and purple clematis sprays

1. Cover each cake with almond paste and champagne sugarpaste as described in the introduction. Cover the large cake drum with sugarpaste. Attach the red velvet ribbon around he base of the drum with non-toxic glue.

2. Centre the largest cake onto the cake drum then stack the two smaller cakes on top. Use the straight-edged sugarpaste smoother to create a neat join between the cakes and the base cake and cake drum, securing it with a few dots of royal icing.

3. Attach a band of ivory ribbon around the base of each cake using a small amount of royal icing to hold it in place at the back of each cake. Decorate the join in the ribbons with a few sugar pearl drags attached again with royal icing.

SIDE DESIGN

4. Bond sheets of edible silver leaf to thinly rolled out white flowerpaste. Leave to dry for about an hour and then use the jasmine leaf paper punch to stamp out several sets of leaves. Attach the leaves at intervals to each of the cakes using a small amount of clear alcohol to secure them. Next, attach pearl dragées to each of the leaf groupings using a piping bag fitted with a No.1 piping tube and filled with royal icing.

5. Insert a posy pick into the top tier and another in the bottom tier. Insert the handles of each spray into the picks to hold them in place. Re-arrange the flowers a little to create a more relaxed setting between the cake and the flowers.

August Bouquet

Deep red velvety roses offset with royal purple clematis flowers, delicate buds and trailing stems of waxy foliage make a lavish and bold arrangement. The spray is simple in its construction, keeping the focus on the flowers.

MATERIALS AND EQUIPMENT
22- and 24-gauge white wires
Nile green floristry tape
Tape shredder
Wire cutters or florist's scissors
Fine-nosed pliers
Antique glass bottle (optional)

FLOWERS AND FOLIAGE
3 full red roses
2 half red roses
3 purple clematis flowers plus buds
9 sets of clematis leaves
7 trailing stems of succulent foliage

1. Tape a 22- or 24-gauge wire onto any of the flower and foliage stems that require extra length or support using ½-width nile green floristry tape.

2. Use the largest full red rose as the starting point for the spray. This will create the focal point and should be higher than the other flowers in the spray. Add other smaller roses around the focal flower using ½-width nile green floristry tape to bind them together.

3. Next, add sets of clematis foliage around the outer edges of the roses using a few sets to create an elongated pointed shape at the tip of the spray.

4. Thread the clematis flowers and buds at intervals around the bouquet and tape these to the other flowers. Trim off any excess bulk wire as you work using wire cutters or sharp floristry scissors. Use the fine-nosed pliers to bend and reshape any of the flower stems that require it to create more movement in the spray.

5. Finally, add the trailing succulent stems to create more length and soften the edges of the display. Here the bouquet is displayed in an old ginger beer bottle.

Sunshine Wedding Cake

Marigolds, like the sunflower turn their heads to follow the sun. They are often known as sun bride, making them a great flower to use for an informal summer wedding cake. Here they provide instant sunshine when offset with contrasting purple clematis flowers.

MATERIALS
13 cm (5 in) and 20 cm (8 in) round fruit cakes (the sunshine fruit cake would be good here) placed on thin boards of the same size
1 kg (2 lb) white almond paste
1.4 kg (3 lb) white sugarpaste
30 cm (12 in) round cake drum
Fine gold spotted purple satin ribbon
Piping bag fitted with a No.1 piping tube and filled with royal icing (optional)
Non-toxic glue stick (Pritt)
Broad brown velvet ribbon

EQUIPMENT
Straight-edge sugarpaste smoother
1 medium and 1 fine food-grade plastic posy pick
Antique (or antique effect) glass cake stand (optional)
Fine-nosed pliers

FLOWERS
1 Tussie Mussie
1 Corsage

1. Cover each cake with almond paste and white sugarpaste following the instructions in the introduction. Cover the large cake drum with white sugarpaste.

2. Centre the large cake on the cake drum and use the straight-edged sugarpaste smoother to blend the join between the base of the cake and the board. Place the smaller cake on the base tier and blend the join using the straight-edged smoother.

3. Attach a fine band of gold spotted purple satin ribbon around the base of each cake using tiny dots of royal icing piped through a No.1 piping tube. Use the non-toxic glue to attach the broad brown velvet ribbon to the edge of the cake drum.

ASSEMBLY

4. Insert the medium-sized posy pick into the top tier and then insert the handle of the Tussie Mussie into it. Insert the finer posy pick into the base of the large tier to hold the corsage.

5. Display the cake on a glass cake stand. Use a pair of fine-nosed pliers to adjust any of the floral elements, as desired.

Tussie-Mussie and Corsage

Orange marigolds and purple clematis are a great combination for a summer wedding. This style of tussie-mussie (posy) was often used by the Victorians. In the 15th century they were known as nosegays - something used as a scent during a smelly era!

1. Tape extra 22-gauge wire onto any of the marigold or clematis flower stems that need extra length or strength using ½-width nile green floristry tape.

ASSEMBLING THE LARGE POSY
2. Group three marigold flowers together, bending their stems to form a snug fit. Tape the three flowers together using ½-width nile green floristry tape. Use wire cutters or sharp florist's scissors to trim off any excess length or bulk wire.

3. Add three purple clematis flowers to fill the gaps between each of the marigolds. Use the groups of clematis buds to soften the edges of the spray.

4. Finally, add the clematis foliage to frame the shape.

SMALL CORSAGE
5. Use ½-width florist tape to bind one marigold flower with three purple clematis flowers. Add a cluster of clematis buds at the front of the corsage and fill in the gaps with clematis foliage.

6. Display the large posy in a small ornate glass vase and rest the corsage at the base.

MATERIALS AND EQUIPMENT
22-gauge white wire
Nile green floristry tape
Wire cutters or sharp florist's scissors
Tape shredder (optional)
Small, ornate glass vase

FLOWERS
4 marigolds
6 purple clematis flowers
3 clusters of clematis buds
10 sets of clematis foliage

White Rose Wedding

White roses, peperomia leaves and trailing stems of hearts entangled foliage trail elegantly down the side of this pretty two-tier wedding cake. The side design is very quick and easy to create using edible rice wafer paper.

MATERIALS
15 cm (6 in) and 20 cm (8 in) rich fruit cakes placed on thin boards of the same size
30 cm (12 in) round cake drum
1.4kg (3 lb 2 oz) white almond paste
1.8 kg (4 lb) white sugarpaste
Narrow soft pink ribbon
Clear alcohol (vodka, kirsch, or Cointreau)
Non-toxic glue stick
Broad soft green ribbon
White rice wafer paper

EQUIPMENT
Sugarpaste smoothers
Curl paper punch (Ww)
1 medium-sized posy pick
Fine-nosed pliers

FLOWERS
White rose and hearts entangled bouquet

1. Cover the cakes and cake drum with almond paste and white sugarpaste. Centre the larger cake on the cake drum and then the smaller cake on top of the large one. While the sugarpaste is still soft blend the joins between the cakes and the cake drum using a straight-edged sugarpaste smoother. Allow to dry overnight.

2. Attach a band of narrow soft pink ribbon around the base of both cakes using a tiny amount of royal icing or sugarpaste softened with clear alcohol and secure the seam at the back. Use non-toxic glue stick to attach a broader band of soft green ribbon to the edge of the cake drum.

RICE PAPER DESIGN
3. Take a sheet of white rice wafer paper and slide into the curl paper punch. Press the lever firmly to make a neat cut. Repeat to cut out enough curls to create a band around both cakes.

4. Lightly moisten the tip of a rice paper curl on the smooth side with clear alcohol and stick in place over the ribbon at the base of a cake. If the rice paper gets too wet it will dissolve. Repeat around the base of both cakes.

ASSEMBLY
5. Insert a medium-sized posy pick into the top tier and insert the handle of the bouquet into the pick to hold it in place. Use fine-nosed pliers to adjust any of the flowers and leaves to create a flowing trail down the side of the cake.

White Rose and Hearts Entangled

I have always loved a white and green colour scheme. Here white roses are combined very simply with a series of heart-shaped foliage - hearts entangled, peperomia and cyclamen leaves each with their own unique texture and decorative markings help to create an interesting trailing bouquet.

MATERIALS AND EQUIPMENT
Tape shredder (optional)
22- or 24-gauge white wire
Nile green floristry tape
Fine-nosed pliers
Wire cutters or sharp florist's scissors
Glass jug (optional)

FLOWERS
Three large white half roses
7 cyclamen leaves
6 trailing stems of hearts
entangled foliage
6 peperomia leaves

1. Cut several lengths of ½-width floristry tape. Strengthen any of the rose or foliage stems that need it by taping 22- or 24-gauge wire onto their main stems using ½-width nile green floristry tape.

ASSEMBLY

2. Take the three white roses and group them together. Use ½-width floristry tape to join their stems together. Use fine-nosed pliers to bend the stems a little to make them sit comfortably together.

3. Use the peperomia leaves to encircle the roses, creating a layered effect as you work. Fine-nosed pliers will be invaluable at this stage to bend the wire stems close to the roses and prevent breakages. Use wire cutters or sharp florist's scissors to trim some of the extra length and bulk that the group of wires will create.

4. Use the cyclamen leaves around the edge of the bouquet and also pull in a leaf behind the focal rose. Use a couple of the leaves to help create a curve and extra length at the front of the bouquet.

5. Use the trailing stems of hearts entangled to create a long trail at the front of the bouquet. Use a few of the remaining stems to curve at the top section. Display the bouquet in a glass vase or jug or keep ready to use on a cake. Use fine-nosed pliers to bend any of the leaf and flower stems that require repositioning.

Snowflakes

There is something soft and delicate about the snowflake. I have used a combination of techniques to create lace-like snowflakes in a design that would be wonderful as a winter wedding cake, a birthday celebration or a rather grand Christmas cake.

MATERIALS

15 cm (6 in) and 20 cm (8 in) rich fruit cakes placed on thin cake boards of the same size
1.4 kg (3 lb 2 oz) white almond paste
1.8 kg (4 lb) white sugarpaste, plus extra for filling the posy picks
30 cm (12 in) round cake drum
Wide and narrow soft peach ribbon
Non-toxic glue stick
Clear alcohol (kirsch, vodka or Cointreau)
White rice wafer paper
White flowerpaste
Small amount of royal icing
Edible white gum arabic glitter flakes
Pearl dragées

EQUIPMENT

Straight-edge sugarpaste smoothers
2 fine food-grade posy picks
Snowflake paper-punch
(MS Martha stewart)
Fine-nosed pliers

DECORATIONS

3 wired snowflakes
Silver paper snowflakes

1. Cover the cakes with almond paste and sugarpaste. Cover the cake drum with sugarpoaste. Centre the small cake on top of the large base tier. While the sugarpaste is still soft blend the bottom edge of the top cake to the larger cake and the larger cake to the cake drum using a straight-edged sugarpaste smoother. Leave to dry overnight.

2. Attach a band of narrow peach ribbon around the base of both cakes using a tiny amount of royal icing or sugarpaste softened with clear alcohol to secure the seam at the back. Use a non-toxic glue stick to attach a broader band of peach ribbon to the edge of the cake drum

ADDING THE SNOWFLAKE DECORATIONS

3. Insert the posy picks into the top tier of the cake. Insert the 'stem' of a snowflake into a pick to hold it in place. You may need to fill the picks with white sugarpaste to give more support. Rest the third snowflake on the base board/cake drum.

4. Use the snowflake paper-punch to cut out some white rice-paper snowflakes as well as white flowerpaste snowflakes. Cut out some edible silver-leaf coated snowflakes too! – see following pages for instructions.

5. Use tiny piped dots of royal icing to secure the various paper-punched sugar snowflakes to the cakes and cake drum. Sprinkle some edible gum arabic 'glitter' flakes over the snowflakes.

Silver Snowflakes

Edible gold and silver leaf adds luxury to a cake design. However, it is expensive and can be tricky to handle. For ease I bond sheets of leaf to a thin layer of flowerpaste, this also reduces wastage. The leftover sections can be kept and broken up into tiny pieces and added to an embroidery or painted side design.

MATERIALS
White vegetable fat
Flowerpaste
Food paste colour
Edible gold (23-carat) or silver leaf
Cornflour dusting bag

EQUIPMENT
Non-stick board and rolling pin
Kitchen paper
Cranked palette knife
Medium paintbrush
Polystyrene dummy cake
Scissors
Snowflake paper-punch (MS)

1. Condition the non-stick board using a small amount of white vegetable fat. Rub into onto the board and then remove with kitchen paper. This prevents paste from sticking and tearing.

2. Roll out some well-kneaded tinted flowerpaste very thinly. I used white. Use a cranked palette knife to release and carefully lift the paste from the board. The side that was on the board should be quite tacky, which helps to bond the paste to the edible gold/silver leaf.

3. Carefully open a book of edible gold or silver leaf. Lower the thinly rolled flowerpaste over the whole sheet of leaf taking care not to cause ripples and air pockets between the two. Use your fingers or a dry and clean medium-sized paintbrush to apply a little pressure to smooth over the paste to help secure the paste to the leaf.

4. Peel back the paste to reveal the coating of leaf. Leave it to set on a polystyrene dummy cake. Trim the excess uncoated paste from the leaf.

5. Place the semi-dried coated flowerpaste into the snowflake paper-punch and press the lever firmly to make a tidy cut. Repeat to cut out the required number of snowflakes.

Wired Snowflakes

These wired sugar snowflakes are great fun to make and could be used as decorations for the Christmas tree and Christmas table. They are fairly quick to make. I have used artistic licence to apply a little colour to the finished snowflakes - they could, of course, be kept white.

MATERIALS
33- and 35-gauge white wires
White floristry tape
White flowerpaste
Fresh egg white (optional)
White pearl sugar dragées
White royal icing
White bridal satin dust
Coral and bluegrass petal dusts
Isopropyl alcohol (kirsch or Cointreau)
Edible spray varnish (Fabilo)
Edible gum arabic 'glitter' flakes

EQUIPMENT
Wire cutters or sharp florist's scissors
Fine-nosed pliers
Tape shredder
Snowflake paper-punch (MS)
No.1 piping tube fitted into a
piping bag

1. Cut several half lengths of 33- or 35-gauge white wire using wire cutters or sharp florists' scissors. Also prepare several lengths of white floristry tape cut into ¼ width using a tape shredder.

2. To make the tips of the snowflakes use soft, well-kneaded white flowerpaste. Add more egg white to your flowerpaste if it feels too firm. Take a length of wire and a tiny ball of flowerpaste and wrap the paste around the end of the dry wire.

3. Hold the wire firmly with one hand and work the paste between your finger and thumb to create a fine strand, removing/pinching off the excess paste at the tip of the wire. Once the strand is fine enough smooth it against your palm. Repeat to make a second strand. Take each section and curve it slightly between your thumb and finger.

4. Using the prepared floristry tape, bind the strands together so that the curves face outwards. This makes one spoke of the snowflake. The length of this section will depend upon the size of snowflake you require. Repeat to make six or eight spokes for each snowflake.

5. Cover the tape with another small piece of well-kneaded white flowerpaste, this time working the paste down the wire between your finger and thumb to create the required length. Repeat on each spoke. Set aside.

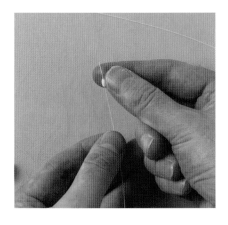
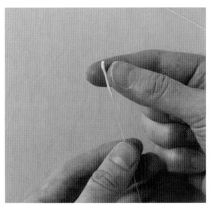
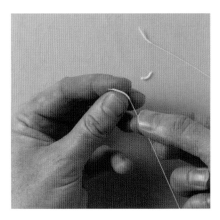

  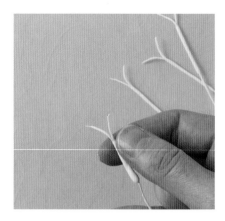

 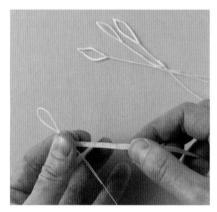 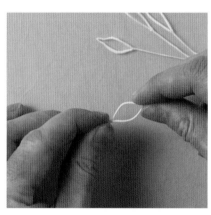

6. Take a length of 33- or 35-gauge white wire and cover the middle section with white flowerpaste to create a long, fine strand. Smooth it between your palms.

7. Create a loop using this section of sugar-coated wire and then hold the two ends of uncoated wire together firmly while you tape them together using ¼-width nile green floristry tape.

8. Pinch the sugar-coated loop into an 'eye' shape using your finger and thumb. Next, add a tiny ball of white flowerpaste to the tip securing it in place with fresh egg white. Repeat to make six or eight sections.

ASSEMBLY

9. Tape the six or eight long 'spokes' together using ¼-width white floristry tape and use fine-nosed pliers to bend each of the wires at an angle to secure them tightly at the centre of the snowflake. Space the spokes evenly and then add the shorter looped sections between each of the long 'spokes' using the pliers to position each of the sections and bend the wires in place. Tape them all together tightly and neatly.

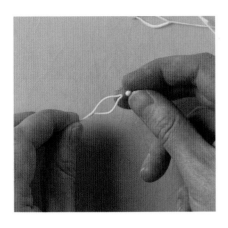

CENTRE

10. The next step is optional, however, it does create extra detail and also tidies the central area. Roll out some white flowerpaste thinly and leave to firm up a little, about 20 minutes. Slide the paste into the snowflake paper-punch and stamp out a snowflake. Attach to the centre of the wired snowflake using a little fresh egg white.

11. Attach a single sugar pearl dragée to the centre of the paper-punched snowflake using a tiny dot of royal icing to secure it in place.

COLOURING

12. Mix together white bridal satin with a touch of coral petal dust and lightly dust the snowflake from the centre fading out towards the edges. Over dust heavily with more white bridal satin.

13. Dilute a light mixture of white bridal satin and bluegrass petal dust with isopropyl alcohol and paint over the sugar pearl dragée at the centre of the snowflake and the tiny balls on the wired looped sections. Spray very lightly with edible spray varnish and then sprinkle with edible gum arabic 'glitter' flakes.

Mariposa Lily Cake

Lilac lilies, love berries, orchids and foliage form the focal point of this fairytale romantic three-tier wedding cake. The colour of the floral display is repeated in the floral side design.

MATERIALS

13 cm (5 in), 18 cm (7 in), and 23 cm (9 in) round fruit cakes placed on thin boards of the same size
White almond paste
White sugarpaste
33 cm (13 in) round cake drum
Fine and broad pale lilac satin ribbon
Small amount of white flowerpaste
Clear alcohol (kirsch or Cointreau)
Plum, African violet, forest, bluegrass and edelweiss white petal dust
Myrtle bridal satin dust
Medium posy pick
Non-toxic glue stick (Pritt)

EQUIPMENT

Sugarpaste smoothers
Non-stick board and rolling pin
Fantasy lily paper-punch (Ww))
Fine paintbrush
Nile green forestry tape
Fine-nosed pliers

FLOWERS

Fairytale romance bouquet
2 Asian ground orchids
3 fantasy blossoms
3 peperomia leaves
1 trailing stem of zebrina

1. Cover the three cakes with almond paste and sugarpaste, then cover the cake drum with sugarpaste following the instructions in the introduction. Centre the two smaller cakes on top of the large base tier and use the sugarpaste smoother to blend the join between the cakes.

2. Attach a narrow band of pale lilac satin ribbon to the bottom of each cake using a small amount of royal icing or sugarpaste softened with clear alcohol to secure it in place. Tie and attach a ribbon bow to cover the join in each ribbon. Use non-toxic glue to secure the broad lilac satin ribbon to the edge of the cake drum.

FLORAL SIDE DESIGN

3. Thinly roll out some white flowerpaste on a non-stick board. Lift the paste from the board and leave to set until it feels like paper.

4. Use the fantasy lily paper-punch to stamp out several sets of flowers. Use a mixture of myrtle satin dust and a touch of forest and bluegrass to create a soft green to dust the leaf section of each of the punched out flowers. Mix together African violet, plum and white to dust the flowers.

5. Attach the cut-out flowers to the sides of the cakes using a little clear alcohol painted onto the backs of the flowers. Add veins using a fine paintbrush and a mixture of African violet and plum petal dust mixed with clear alcohol.

FLORAL CAKE TOP

6. Insert a medium posy pick into the top tier, and insert the handle of the fairytale romance bouquet into it. Use fine-nosed pliers to adjust the flowers and foliage.

7. Tape 2 Asian ground orchids together alongside a trailing stem of zebrina. Add 3 peperomia leaves. Thread in the three fantasy blossoms and tape to tidy the spray handle. This spray simply rests against the base board.

Mariposa Lily Spray

Mariposa lilies form an interesting focal point in this curved trailing spray. The ornate markings of the tradescantia and peperomia leaves add interest and strong colour, while the orchids and berries soften the edges of the display.

1. Use a tape shredder to cut lengths of ½-width or ¼-width nile green floristry tape.

2. If any of the flowers or foliage need extra length or support tape extra wire onto their stems using ½-width tape. I would use 22-gauge wire here.

ASSEMBLY

3. For the large spray, take two trailing stems of tradescantia foliage (one slightly longer than the other) and bend their stems to a 90° angle using fine-nosed pliers. Hold the stems together and tape them using the prepared floristry tape. Visualise the spray in sections. Generally, the focal area takes two-thirds of the spray and the remaining third sits above the focal area ascending to its tip.

4. Stretch the tape as you bind the stems together, this releases the glue in the tape and enables it to stick to itself. Hold the tape pulling tightly at an angle and with one hand and turn the stem with the other hand. Break off any excess tape between stages. This creates a 'handle' to the spray/bouquet and it is from this point that I add all the other flowers and foliage.

5. Next, add the focal flower. In this instance a mariposa lily. The lily should be larger and stand slightly higher than any other flower in the spray/bouquet. Tape the flower tightly in place.

MATERIALS AND EQUIPMENT
Tape shredder
Nile green floristry tape
22-gauge white wires
Fine nosed pliers
Wire cutters or sharp florist's scissors
Small glass vase (optional)

FLOWERS AND FOLIAGE
  (LARGE SPRAY)
5 stems of tradescantia foliage
2 mariposa lilies
3 sets of love berries
3 Asian ground orchids
3 fantasy blossoms
5 peperomia leaves

(SMALL SPRAY)
2 Asian ground orchids
3 fantasy bossom
3 peperomia leaves
1 stems of tradescantia

6. Add the shorter stems of tradescantia to create the basic outline of the spray and fill in the large space at the outer curve of the spray. Add the second mariposa lily to one side of the focal flower. In commercial floristry the guideline for using flowers in odd numbers is often followed quite strictly, so you might prefer a third lily in this spray. In Japanese Ikebana and freestyle floristry this rule is not always followed, and I sometimes find that two flowers give enough presence in a spray.

7. Use the stems of love berries opposite each other in the spray running a diagonal line through the display. Tape them in using ½-width floristry tape. As you work you might find that the increasing number of wires creates too much bulk, so trim off some of the excess wire using sharp scissors or wire cutters.

8. Add the three Asian ground orchids to fill in more space, spreading them evenly through the spray, then add the three fantasy blossoms slightly recessed and evenly spaced to add a little more depth to the spray.

9. Use the large peperomia leaves to frame the spray and fill in the large gaps left by the trailing tradescantia foliage. Use full-width floristry tape to tidy the spray's handle.

SMALL SPRAY

10. Tape two Asian ground orchids to the base of a trailing stem of tradescantia foliage using ½-width floristry tape. Next, add the three fantasy blossom evenly spaced around the orchids. Finally add the peperomia leaves to frame the flowers. Display in a glass vase.

Tattoodium

Yes, I know it's an odd name for a cake! This cake was commissioned and created for an after-show party at the London Palladium theatre for three of the original members of Eurovision Song Contest winner Bucks Fizz!

MATERIALS

20 cm (8 in) elliptical polystyrene dummy cake (optional, see step 1)
30 cm (12 in) gum leaf-shaped rich fruit cake placed on a thin cake board of the same size
White almond paste
White sugarpaste
Bright orange satin ribbon
Fine pale aqua ribbon
White flowerpaste
Cocoa butter
Clear alcohol
Bluegrass, African violet, blue, plum, tangerine, coral, edelweiss white petal dusts
Edible gold powder food colour (SK)
2 medium posy picks

EQUIPMENT

Non-stick board and rolling pin
Butterfly wing templates
Sharp craft knife or plain-edge cutting wheel (PME)
Heart-shaped cutters or templates
Assorted paintbrushes
Fine scriber or ballpoint pen that has run out of ink
Cup and saucer
Straight-edge sugarpaste smoother
Perspex tilting cake stand (CC)
Long corsage pins

FLOWERS

2 exotic gerbera sprays
3 stems ornamental yam leaves

1. I use a dummy cake for the top tier and provide extra cake to share, if needed. Coat the dummy with sugarpaste. Cover the fruit cake with almond paste and then with sugarpaste. Coat the cake drum with sugarpaste. Centre the fruit cake on the cake drum. Leave the dummy to dry for several days and the cake to dry overnight.

2. Attach orange ribbon to the bottom of the dummy using a small amount of royal icing. Stick the same ribbon to the edge of the cake drum using non-toxic glue. Secure the aqua ribbon to the bottom edge of the large cake.

FANTASY BUTTERFLY TATTOO DESIGN (TOP TIER)

3. Roll out some well-kneaded white flowerpaste on a non stick board. Use the templates from the back of the book and a sharp craft knife to cut out the wings and body sections of the butterfly. Cut out a heart using a heart cutter.

4. Attach the pieces to the dummy cake using clear alcohol. Position the wings first then the abdomen, main body and finally the head. Attach the heart at the top of the cake directly above the butterfly's head.

5. Paint the detail on the butterfly and the various design elements freehand or trace the designs and then scribe them onto the surface using a fine scriber.

6. Melt some cocoa butter onto a saucer placed on a cup filled with just boiled water. Mix petal dusts mixed into the cocoa butter to create a painting medium. Start by outlining the sections of the butterfly wings, the eye detail and the body using African violet and a touch of edelweiss petal dust. Allow the colour to set before adding other colours.

7. Mix bluegrass, edelweiss and a touch of blue petal dust with melted cocoa butter to paint in the intense eye colour and the upper part of the abdomen. Add extra white petal dust to the mix for the lower wings, fading the colour slightly towards the middle of each wing, and also to paint in the antennae. Paint the feathered wings above the cut-out heart in the same colour.

8. Mix some plum petal dust with a tiny amount of edelweiss and cocoa butter. Use to paint the strong pink markings on the lower wings, the scalloped design on the edge of the wings, the outline of the fuchsia flower, its stamens at the base of the abdomen, and the hearts to the right of the design. Add extra edelweiss petal dust to the mixture and colour the upper sections of the butterfly wings taking care to avoid the eye design. The colour should be intense at the the base of the wings fading out slightly about half way through the shape. Allow the paintwork to set a little.

9. Mix some tangerine, edelweiss and a touch of plum into melted cocoa butter. Add brush strokes to the fuchsia flower, the hearts and the main body section. Allow to set and then increase the amount of tangerine and plum to add extra detail.

10. Mix in some aubergine petal dust and paint the butterfly's head. Add extra depth to the eye area as well as some detail spotting at the tips of each wing and the tips of the fuchsia stamens. Finally, mix a little gold powder food colour into the cocoa butter to add gold highlights to the wings and the hearts. Allow to dry.

BOTTOM TIER

11. Roll out some more well-kneaded white flowerpaste and cut out five hearts. Moisten the back of each with clear alcohol and attach at intervals on the top left-hand edge of the cake curving down onto the front side of the cake. Continue painting in the various sections of the design using the colours used in the butterfly design. Paint the lips, champagne flutes and the eye directly onto the cake. Finally add the gold highlights.

ASSEMBLY

12. Place the perspex tilting stand onto of the coated cake board at the back of the bottom tier. Carefully position the top tier onto the tilt of the stand (it is good to have an extra pair of hands at this stage!) and quickly insert a few long corsage pins through the holes in the stand and into the base of the dummy cake to hold it in place.

13. Insert a medium-sized posy pick into the top edge of the top tier and insert the handle of the gerbera spray into it curling and curving the trail of the spray around the left-hand edge of the cake and the base of the perspex stand. Insert the second posy pick into the base tier to hold the second spray of flowers. Use fine-nosed pliers to adjust the arrangement to create a flowing design. Add the extra trailing stems of ornamental yam leaves to trail around the back of the perspex stand.

Exotic Party Spray

The strong colours used in the tattoo designs of the Tattoodium cake have been echoed in these vibrant and quite unusual sprays of flowers. Orange flamboyant flowers are used to frame the more delicate coral gerbera flowers and a cooling aqua note is added using the florists sisal covered wire to complete the design.

MATERIALS AND EQUIPMENT
22-gauge white wires
Nile green floristry tape
Florists' aqua sisal-covered wire
Tape shredder
Orange decorative paper-covered wire
Clear glass vase

FLOWERS AND FOLIAGE
6 trails of ornamental yam leaves
2 pale coral gerbera flowers
5 orange flamboyant flowers
4 large pink Asian ground orchids

1. Add extra length and strength to any of the flowers and foliage, as required, by taping 22-gauge white wire to them using ½-width floristry tape.

ASSEMBLY

2. Add three trailing stems of ornamental yam leaves around a large coral gerbera using ½-width floristry tape. One of the trailing stems of yam should be longer to trail at the base of the spray. Trim any excess wire. Curve the trailing stems to form a reversed 's' shape.

3. Tightly tape in three flamboyant flowers around the gerbera to create a strong band of orange; don't worry if the petals overlap slightly.

4. Use lengths of the aqua sisal-covered and orange paper-covered wire to add a trailing tangle to the spray. Secure using ½-width floristry tape.

5. Add two large pink Asian ground orchids positioning them on each side of the central gerbera to create a line of pink and coral running through the design. Repeat to make a second spray. Display in a clear glass vase.

Exotic Splash

This fabulous and bold piece of work was created for a competition. The maker has kindly allowed me to use her arrangement. There is a maritime theme to this piece - Drunken sailor flowers, cannonball flower and coral stranded on driftwood - a very clever piece of work!

1. Strengthen any of the flower stems that need it by taping 20- or 22-gauge white wire onto their stems using ½–width nile green floristry tape.

2. Secure the driftwood to the glass plate using photographers' strong black tack.

ASSEMBLY

3. Attach some florist's brown staysoft to the back of the driftwood. It should stick without help, however, you might prefer to use some craft glue.

4. Bend a hook in the end of the stem of the cannonball flower, this will help give extra support to the flower in the arrangement. Insert the hooked stem of the flower into the staysoft to form the focal point of the arrangement.

5. Make a hook at the end of two stems of drunken sailor vine. Use the longest piece at the right-hand side of the arrangement and the shorter piece opposite to form an almost reversed 's' shape. Use fine-nosed pliers to bend and position the flowers and leaves and the main stem too.

6. Finally, hook the stems of the five pieces of coral and take care when arranging the flowers. Use the pliers to bend and move the main stems to help and add a little 'movement' to the piece.

MATERIALS AND EQUIPMENT
20- and 22-gauge white wires
Nile green floristry tape
A piece of natural driftwood
Clear green glass plate
Wire cutters or sharp florist's scissors
Photographer's strong black tack
Brown florists' staysoft
Craft glue
Fine-nosed pliers

FLOWERS AND FOLIAGE
1 shivalinga flower
1 large and 1 smaller stem of drunken sailor flowers and foliage
5 pieces of coral

Exotica Bouquet

Exotic orange flamboyant flowers form the focal point of this vibrant display, which has an almost Indian vibe. Trailing tradescantia foliage, purple clematis and orange marigolds complement each other in this curved creative bouquet.

MATERIALS AND EQUIPMENT
22-gauge white wires
Nile green floristry tape
Tape shredder
Fine-nosed pliers
Wire cutters or sharp florist's scissors
Clear glass vase

FLOWERS AND FOLIAGE
5 trailing stems clematis leaves with 3 sets of buds and 6 clematis flowers
3 orange flamboyant flowers
3 marigold flowers 3 trailing stems of tradescantia

1. Add extra strength and length to any of the flowers and foliage as necessary by taping 22-gauge wire onto their stems using ½-width floristry tape.

ASSEMBLY

2. Use the stems of the clematis leaves with flowers to form the length and width of the bouquet. Start with one long length, which should be about two thirds of the length of the whole spray. Bend the end of the stem to a 90° angle and add a slightly shorter stem directly opposite. Tape them together using ½-width floristry tape. Next add the shorter stems of clematis foliage and flowers to form the width of the bouquet. Trim any bulky stems.

3. Add and tape in the three flamboyant flowers to creates the focal area. One of the flowers should be centred and stand slightly proud of the other two.

4. Use the marigold flowers to fill in around the flamboyant flowers. Add the trailing stems of tradescantia to curve through the edges of the bouquet taping them one by one with ½-width floristry tape. Trim any excess wire.

5. Use fine-nosed pliers to bend and re-position any of the flowers and foliage that need adjusting. Display in a clear green glass vase.

Templates

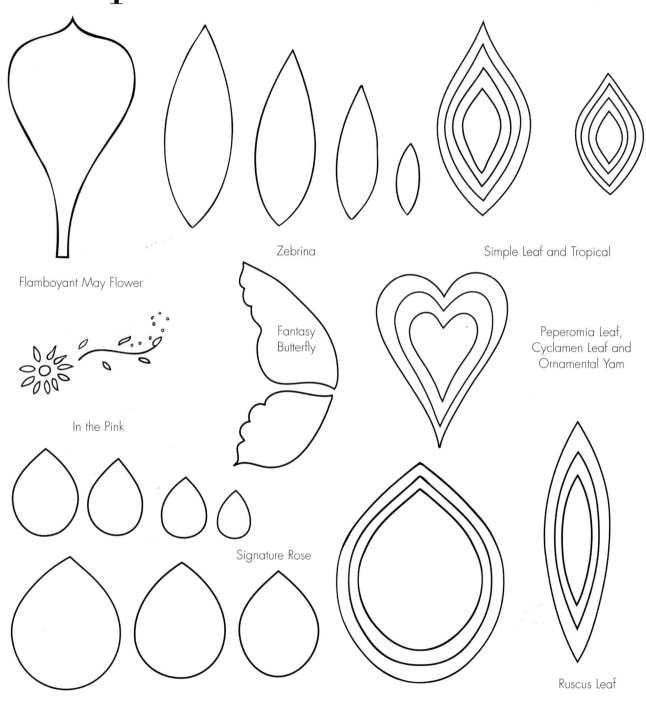

Flamboyant May Flower

Zebrina

Simple Leaf and Tropical

In the Pink

Fantasy
Butterfly

Peperomia Leaf,
Cyclamen Leaf and
Ornamental Yam

Signature Rose

Ruscus Leaf

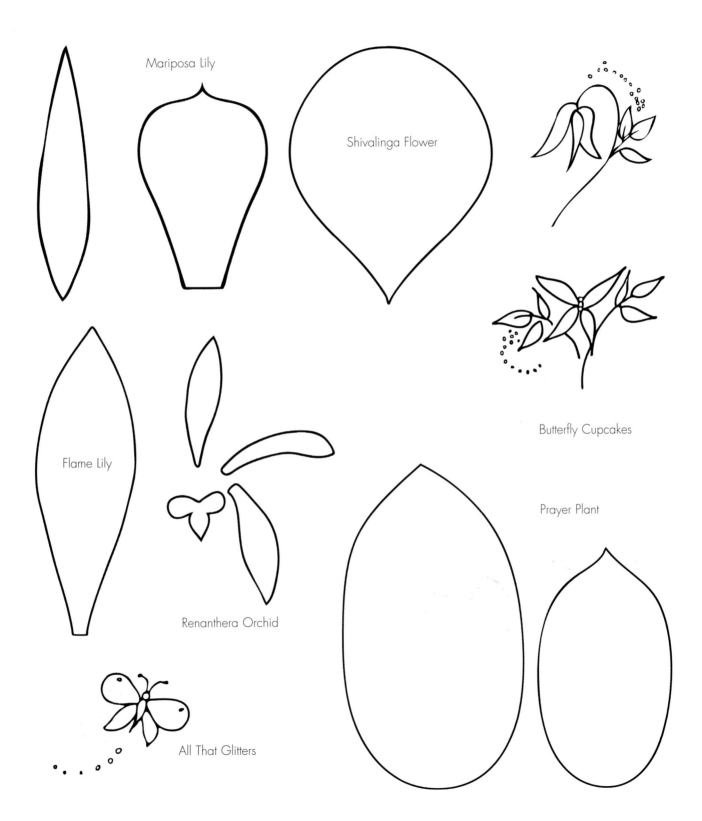

Mariposa Lily

Shivalinga Flower

Butterfly Cupcakes

Flame Lily

Prayer Plant

Renanthera Orchid

All That Glitters

Tattoodium

Suppliers

A Piece of Cake (APOC)
18 Upper High Street
Thame
Oxon OX9 3EX
01844 213428
www.sugaricing.com

Aldaval Veiners (ALDV)
16 Chibburn Court
Widdrington
Morpeth
Northumberland NE61 5QT
+44 (0)1670 790 995

Celcakes and Celcrafts (CC)
Springfield House
Gate Helmsley
York YO4 1NF
www.celcrafts.co.uk

Celebrations
Unit 383 G
Jedburgh Court
Team Valley Trading Estate
Gateshead
Tyne and Wear NE11 0BQ
www.celebrations-teamvalley.co.uk

Culpitt Cake Art
Jubilee Industrial Estate
Ashington
Northumberland
NE63 8UG
www.culpitt.com

Design-a-Cake
30/31 Phoenix Road
Crowther Industrial Estate
Washington
Tyne & Wear NE38 0AD
www.design-a-cake.co.uk

Guy, Paul & Co Ltd
(UK distributor for Jem cutters)
Unit 10 The Business Centre
Corinium Industrial estate
Raans Road
Amersham
Buckinghamshire HP6 6FB
www.guypaul.co.uk

Holly Products (HP)
Primrose Cottage
Church Walk
Norton in Hales
Shropshire TF9 4QX
www.hollyproducts.co.uk

Orchard Products (OPR)
51 Hallyburton Road
Hove, East Sussex
BN3 7GP
www.orchardproducts.co.uk

The British Sugarcraft Guild
Wellington House
Messeter Place
Eltham
London SE9 5DP
www.bsguk.org

The Old Bakery
Kingston St Mary
Taunton
Somerset TA2 8HW
www.oldbakery.co.uk

Tinkertech Two (TT)
40 Langdon Road
Parkstone
Poole
Dorset BH14 9EH

Squires Kitchen (SKGI)
Squires House
3 Waverley Lane
Farnham
Surrey GU9 8BB
www.squires-shop.com

The Stencil Library
Stocksfield Hall
Stocksfield
Northumberland
NE43 7TN
Tel: +44 (0)1661 844 844

EUROPE
Ellen's Creative Cakes
Atelier: Norgerweg 208
9497PH Donderen
Netherlands
www.ellenscreativecakes.nl

Flower Veiners
Boetonstraat 8-H
1095 XL Amsterdam
E-mail: info@flowerveiners.nl

AUSTRALIA
My Cake Delights
219 High Street
Preston 3072
Melbourne
www.mycakedelights.com

Contact the author
www.alandunnsugarcraft.com